D0392473

BATTLE FOR AFRICA

BY Brother Andrew

God's Smuggler (with John and Elizabeth Sherrill)
Battle for Africa (with Charles Paul Conn)

BY Charles Paul Conn

The New Johnny Cash
Hooked on a Good Thing (with Sammy Hall)
No Easy Game (with Terry Bradshaw)
Just Off Chicken Street (with Floyd McClung)
Believe! (with Richard M. DeVos)
The Magnificent Three (with Nicky Cruz)
Julian Carroll of Kentucky
The Possible Dream
Battle for Africa (with Brother Andrew)

BROTHER ANDREW
WITH CHARLES PAUL CONN

Battle for Africa

Fleming H. Revell Company
Old Tappan, New Jersey

Scripture quotations in this volume are from the King James Version of the Bible.

Library of Congress Cataloging in Publication Data

Andrew, Brother.
Battle for Africa.

1. Christianity—Africa. 2. Communism and Christianity—Africa. I. Conn, Charles Paul, joint author. II. Title.
BR1360.A57 209'.6 77-13280
ISBN 0-8007-0876-8

Published by Fleming H. Revell Company

Printed in the United States of America

For we wrestle not against flesh and blood, but against principalities, against powers, against the rulers of the darkness of this world, against spiritual wickedness in high places.

Ephesians 6:12

Contents

Foreword

It's been ten years since *God's Smuggler* was published—and nearly one million copies have been sold. Brother Andrew's story of those who risk their lives to bring the Word to worshipers cut off from the Scriptures behind the Iron Curtain is an incredible account of faith and courage.

Yet a young Andrew did not start out with such a mission. He was a mischievous youth and played hooky from church and tricks on the invading Nazis in Witte, Holland, where he was born. At seventeen he went off to war in Indonesia as a commando. Andrew had a suicidal bravado in combat, was frequently drunk and—at last—full of self-disgust.

Wounded and soul-weary, he found the Lord and his own particular mission as God's smuggler—carrying Bibles for the spiritually isolated. His famed prayer thrilled thousands of readers: "When You were on earth, You made blind eyes see. Now, I pray, make seeing eyes blind. Do not let the guards see those things You do not want them to see."

For the past three years, more and more of his ministry has been aimed at Africa—and its suffering church. Yes, the Revolution has come to that vast, troubled continent. You need only read the newspapers to know what turmoil is taking place in Africa. Does it affect us here in America? Can we do anything about it? To these questions, Brother Andrew has answers—and a burden for every Christian.

We, at Fleming H. Revell Company, are proud to present this important book.

THE PUBLISHERS

BATTLE FOR AFRICA

1

From Angola to Zambia—A Giant Battleground

Africa is a giant battlefield.

The headlines of newspapers around the world shout out the agonies of a continent in turmoil:

- In Zaire, invading troops from neighboring Angola storm across the Katanga province, are pushed back, then attack again . . . .
- In Uganda, a hand-grenade attack on dictator Idi Amin Dada fails, killing ten bystanders instead . . . .
- In Angola, a vicious civil war rages, with thousands of Cubans fighting on the side of the victorious MPLA revolutionaries . . . .
- In Madagascar, one thousand civilians are killed, as laborers fight one another in an outbreak of tribal warfare . . . .
- In Malawi, six thousand Asians are expelled from the country without explanation . . . .
- In Mozambique, reports continue of a heightening campaign of repression against the Christian church . . . .

- In Rhodesia, terrorists line up twenty-seven unarmed farm workers and shoot them to death during Christmas festivities . . . .
- In South Africa, riots break out in black townships, with police jailing an undisclosed number of citizens, mostly young people, in mass arrests . . . .
- In Burundi, the ten-year-old regime of President Micambero is overthrown by a military coup . . . .
- In Equatorial Guinea, nearly a quarter of the population become refugees, fleeing a government that has reportedly made slaves of over twenty thousand civilians . . . .
- In Ethiopia, there is another assassination attempt, following a day of demonstration and violence in the nation's capital, with scores of people killed . . . .

There it is—just a sample of today's Africa—enough bloodshed and upheaval to last a decade—all packed into a three-month period late last year!

Africa has been a violent and dangerous land since the first explorers pushed into what was then called the *Dark Continent.* But the Africa of today is not just a remote, strange place where men of primitive cultures wage their own private wars. It has become much more than that. It has become the scene of the most important struggle on the face of the globe—a battle between the forces of God and the forces of evil. The battle for Africa is on; and, like it or not, *every one of us* will emerge individually from that battle as winner or loser.

I am going to urge you in this book to join in the battle for Africa, but admittedly not for any lofty or unselfish motive.

We who sit in comfortable lands thousands of miles away from Africa must get involved in the fight for our *own* survival's sake. What does Africa have to do with us? Everything! A Revolution has come to Africa, and if it overwhelms that continent, it will move on to a closer battleground. Its ultimate target is you and every person you love and hold dear. Its ultimate goal is the eradication of all that is good and beautiful. We will be its victor, or every one of us will eventually be its victim.

A Spiritual Battle

To say there is a battle for Africa suggests that great powers are locked in a fight, with Africa as the prize. That is true politically, economically, militarily, and racially. But those are not the battles which should most interest us. Those battles we leave to politicians, generals, and economists. The battle for Africa that we must join is a *spiritual* battle, and that is the most critical battle of all.

I believe there is only one basic conflict in Africa. Politicians don't have the guts to cope with it, the sense to accept it, the moral power to make decisions that will resolve it. That is the *spiritual* conflict of the church, with all it stands for, against the Revolution, with all that it includes. Seeing the African situation from that perspective doesn't solve the problems there. It gives no pat, pious answers. The battle still must be won with sheer hard work, prayer, and getting back to the basics of the Great Commission. But at least seeing Africa as a spiritual battlefield is a place to start. At least it provides a valid point from which to understand the situation and attack the problem.

If we accept the African struggle as a spiritual one, then we can believe that it matters what we know and do. Satan would like us to believe that the battle will be decided by armies and governments, by generals and diplomats. But that is not true. The battle is a *spiritual* one, and in a spiritual battle the critical weapons are prayer, intercession, and the commitment of Christians all around the world. *You* can make a difference in Africa! Absurd as it sounds, it is nevertheless true. If the battle is a spiritual one, if the solutions are spiritual ones, then *you,* individually—right from where you live—can make a difference in the fate of Africa!

All we do *must be* based on the faith that it is not too late to change the course of Africa. We must not be fatalistic. We *must* believe that individual Christians can intervene in the course of world events and change the course of history. What happens is determined not by some kind of predetermined, inevitable fate. What happens is determined by *your* faith, *your* actions, *your* will, *your* love, *your* willingness to take up a spiritual burden and bear it before the Lord.

We must not be spectators in the battle! We can be involved—as surely as any diplomat or statesman—as powerfully as any soldier—in the outcome in Africa. We have a choice. We can sit by and watch Africa collapse under the Revolution; or we can find out what is going on, and get serious with God about how we can help.

That's what this book is all about.

2

The Suffering Church

As I share my burden for Africa, I can almost see the question form in the minds of those who read this book: "How in the world," you will ask, "did Brother Andrew get from his Bible-smuggling ministry in Eastern Europe to the continent of Africa?"

That is a fair question, and the answer is a rather interesting one. When I wrote my first book (exactly ten years ago), I was deeply, personally involved in taking Bibles behind the Iron Curtain, and that ministry was the story the book told. I became known as "God's smuggler," from the book's title, and I have discovered that many people still think of me as I was in those days, driving through Communist checkpoints in a Volkswagen, with a load of Bibles packed in the rear. What I am doing now is not nearly so different as some people might think. The main differences are the color of the skin and the names on the road signs.

I have never thought of my work as being a "smuggling" ministry. God didn't call me to smuggle; He called me to minister to His people. It just happens that many of His people are in countries with walls and fences and border blockades to keep them in and me out. So ministering to them necessarily involved a bit of challenge, yes, even breaking the law in some countries. So I did that. And when I visited people in those countries, I found that their greatest need was for Bibles to read. "What can I do for you?" I asked them. "Please bring us Bibles," they replied. And so I did. For fifteen years I took them Bibles and other Christian literature. God helped me. He closed the eyes of border guards more times than I can remember, performed more miracles than I can tell; and consequently, I took Bibles to people behind the Iron Curtain for years without spending a single night in jail. Why? Simply because God intends for His children to have His Word, and some man named Stalin or Khrushchev or Brezhnev is certainly not going to interfere with that.

When the book describing my activities was published, it changed things. People all around the world became aware of their responsibility to minister to Christians in restricted areas. I call this segment of the Kingdom the *suffering church.* I do not call it the *underground church* because that term, to me, suggests a group of people hiding somewhere with no active witness for the Lord—and the Christians I have met don't fit that description at all. I do not refer to it as the church in *closed countries* because I do not believe that any country is truly closed to the Gospel. God simply will not allow it! Some areas are more difficult to get into than others. Some require greater sacrifice and entail greater danger. But all doors are open if we shove on them hard enough. There is no country closed to the church, but certainly there are places where the church pays for its existence with great suffering.

My ministry is to that suffering church anywhere in the world, but in the last half of the twentieth century, the sharp increase in the number of suffering Christians has grown in direct proportion to the spread of the worldwide Revolution. Whether it comes under the name of communism or nationalism or liberation or whatever, the result is still the same: wherever the Revolution gains control, the church is one of the first casualties. It was in Eastern Europe that the Revolution first began to wage war against the church—in Russia and Poland, in East Germany, and Romania, in all the other countries that came under Communist control by the end of World War II. And it was the suffering church of Eastern Europe which I first met and ministered to.

When *God's Smuggler* came out, hundreds of thousands of Christians who had never thought seriously about the suffering church began to pray for their brothers and sisters in Communist lands. People began to offer themselves personally to help in the ministry. Amazing things happened. An accountant in New Zealand, for example, was sent to London on a business trip. He traveled by way of Siberia, hauling Bibles with him as he went, leaving them at stops along the way. He wrote me, jubilantly, when he reached London, saying, "God did the same miracles for me that He did for you!"

There were many similar cases. One of my misgivings about writing the book had been the argument that it would alert the Communist authorities, and they would make things more difficult. But even that turned out to be a blessing! As there was more opposition to what we were doing, there were more prayers prayed, hence more miracles worked, hence more victories won! That book became one giant prayer-letter! The small stream of Christian literature which I could personally account for grew to a virtual flood as more and more Christians got involved in the work.

Open Doors

My dream of dozens of teams of tourists, students, families, and businessmen moving across the borders with small loads of Bibles became a reality. The organization which now supervises these activities is called Open Doors; and from its base in Ermelo, Holland, we send out eighty to one hundred teams a year to minister to the suffering church. We work hard to weed out the adventure-seekers and irresponsible volunteers, and to train the people who go into restricted areas. We never take unnecessary risks. We never send people out unprepared for what they will face. And so far, by the grace of God, we have never had a team imprisoned. We have had some very close calls. We have had to spend lots of time in prayer for teams that seemed to be in trouble. But so far everyone who has gone in has come out again.

We train people to go into strange places where they don't know Christians and find them. Veteran workers go into difficult areas on "information trips" to make contacts, set up distribution systems, find out what specific things the churches in various towns need, and generally pave the way for the larger numbers of teams that come in with the tourist flood. We purchased property and equipment to customize vehicles, rebuilding them to carry up to seven or eight hundred Bibles.

The upshot of all this is that we are getting more Bibles into controlled countries now than ever before, as well as ministering in other ways. We took an entire printing press into one town, have taken several automobiles for the work of local ministers, and have conducted thousands of prayer meetings and worship services. There is one small Russian town, for instance, where in the past ten years we have taken over twelve thousand Bibles (most of which were, of course, passed on to believers in needier areas).

But one negative outcome of the publishing of *God's Smuggler* has been that I eventually was forced to stop my own personal involvement in these trips. I didn't quit immediately; but, within a year or so of the publication of the book, I began to receive evidence that the police were aware of my specific trips, and were watching closely to see whom I visited and met with while inside their countries. I finally stopped going personally, when friends in Eastern Europe sent word that they had been called in for questioning and had seen a copy of *God's Smuggler* on the officer's desk in the police station! That was enough to convince me that, after fifteen years in the foxholes, it was time for me to retire to the strategy room, and leave the more exciting side of things to persons less well known to the authorities.

Meeting Them Halfway

One of the last literature runs I made was a trip to Prague, Czechoslovakia, when the Soviet army invaded that city in 1968. A week before the Russians moved into Czechoslovakia, I had a strange feeling that somehow it would happen, and predicted the invasion to a friend a week before it actually occurred. One day I was in my office here in Holland, and my children burst in, shouting that the television news was on with reports from Prague. I turned on a set just in time to see a live report from Czechoslovakia describing the Soviet invasion.

When I saw that on television, I didn't need a prayer meeting to tell me what to do. I figured if the Russians were coming to meet me halfway, I'd better get moving!

That afternoon I loaded my station wagon with Russian Bibles and drove from Holland to the Czech border in one day. I didn't even bother to hide the Bibles, counting on the confusion (which I knew I would find) to get me past the border without a vehicle search. When I got to the border, there was a line of cars over a mile long, thousands of Czechs waiting to get out. I was the only one going the other way. As I had expected, the harried Czech border patrol officer didn't even ask for a visa, much less check my car. He just looked at me like I was crazy, slowly shook his head, stamped my passport, and waved me through.

Six miles past the border, I almost literally ran into the Soviet army. I rounded a curve and saw two huge tanks blocking the road. A Russian soldier came to the car, a frown stretched across his face, and asked to see my papers. As I handed them to him through the car window, I prayed the Smuggler's Prayer that I had prayed so often before: "Lord, in my luggage I have Scripture that I want to take to Your children across this border. When You were on earth, You made blind eyes see. Now, I pray, make seeing eyes blind. Do not let the guards see those things You do not want them to see." And once again God honored—and answered—the prayer. The soldiers didn't even look inside the station wagon. They let me through.

Several miles farther I encountered another army division in the town of Pilzen. Somehow I got in the middle of a long column of Soviet tanks, rumbling down the main street of Pilzen. It was a very strange experience, and an embarrassing one, because thousands of people lined the streets and squares of that town, all shaking their fists and looking angrily at the Russians, spitting in our direction. They were a quiet crowd, dead quiet. But when they saw my station wagon with Dutch registration plates, they began shouting and cheering. I thought, "Oh, please, don't do that. This is no time to give a warm welcome to a poor Dutchman! Not with a Russian tank five yards behind me!" Gradually I passed the tanks and was on the open road again rolling toward Prague. Many people stopped me and warned me not to go to Prague, which by that time was fully occupied. I arrived there that evening.

The city was a mess. Czech citizens had turned all the road signs around, had painted over all the street names and house numbers to confuse the Russians. Hastily made signs taunted the Russians and pointed the way to Moscow. I preached in a church that Sunday morning. Tanks were grinding through the streets; shooting could be heard sporadically in the distance; yet the church was packed with a standing-room-only crowd. During that sermon, I stressed the theme: "If you do not go to the heathen with the Gospel, they will come to you as revolutionaries or as occupying forces." At the end of the service I stood at the door shaking hands, and they almost crushed my fingers, thanking me emotionally for coming to minister to them.

I challenged the people in the church that morning to seize the opportunity to evangelize the Russian soldiers, and dumped my load of Bibles on a table in front of the church. They took them—all of them—and went out to give the occupational Soviet troops the Scriptures. The Soviet soldiers were an unhappy lot. They had been told that they would be received warmly, as liberating friends, by the Czechs. Instead they found hostile, bitter citizens who cursed them, threw rocks at them, even tried to set fire to their tanks. They were scared stiff, and totally demoralized. Then suddenly that Sunday morning smiling Czech people came to them, saying, "Ivan, Jesus loves you. Here's a book that tells you about it!" And they gave them those Bibles in their own Russian language. "We love you because Jesus loves you," they told the Russian soldiers. This happened not only in Prague, but in other cities where we had sent teams.

After that we went through Prague giving out tracts to Czech civilians. We had never had it so easy. The Czech citizens took them, and Bibles which we distributed, like starving men taking bread. Czech authorities were too busy coping with the Russians to worry about arresting us, and we gave away tens of thousands of tracts before we finally depleted our supply, and I headed back for Holland. That was one of my last personal literature trips. I did take a load into Yugoslavia a couple of years after that, I confess, but it was an easy run and I decided I deserved one last trip!

The Asian Struggle

During the 1960s, the scene of the great Revolutionary struggle shifted from Eastern Europe to Southeast Asia.

There should be nothing surprising about a shift of this sort, if one takes the Communists seriously. Since the original Bolshevik Revolution in Russia in 1917, the declared goal of the Revolution has been world domination, and there has never been an indication that such plans have changed. Eastern Europe fell like a tired prizefighter into the Soviet camp after World War II. A few years were required to establish the European regimes, and there were a few uprisings—especially in Hungary and Poland—to squash. But by the mid-1960s, Eastern Europe had become an apparently secure area for the Revolution, and the focus of the struggle became Southeast Asia.

The terminology may be a bit different in Asia than in Eastern Europe, but the battle is the same one. The major force there is China; the ideological keynote is *nationalism;* the emotional issue is food for hungry masses of Asians. But those are mere details. The real struggle in Asia was the struggle of the church to survive under repressive regimes that threatened to stamp out Christianity altogether. The Revolution spread like a prairie fire across Southeast Asia in the 1960s, and the first casualty, as always, was the church.

My first trip to Red China was in 1965, and there I discovered a suffering church so similar to that in Europe that I had the feeling I had seen it all before. I went from China to Vietnam, sensing that the Revolution was somehow irresistibly spreading through that land. I was in Da Nang on the day the U.S. Marines landed, and watched them come ashore to begin the long, horrible, futile war which they were destined to lose eight years later. They lost because they were never determined to win; they did not even plan to win. After that I spent a month in Vietnam each year, working with the soldiers as well as with the tribesmen of the mountain region, and with the Vietnamese churches. I could see that the Communists would eventually prevail, and wanted desperately to prepare the Christians I had met for the suffering which they are enduring today. Even in the early, optimistic days, the pulse and flow of Southeast Asia was moving irresistibly in the direction of the Revolutionaries.

"It is not weapons that decide the outcome of a war," Chairman Mao once said, "but the men who carry the weapons." I thought of that statement many times as I saw the Viet Cong, with single-minded commitment to their cause, moving up and down the Ho Chi Minh Trail by foot, carrying heavy equipment and material on their backs, living on tiny bags of rice, dedicated to some vision of a Communist Vietnam. I compared the hardship of those people to the Americans, with all their numbers and expensive weapons, their hardware and technology, but with confused, ambivalent soldiers, who were sensitive to lack of support back home, and simply eager to get it over with and get out of there.

In the middle sixties, the Communists had more full-time literature distributors in Southeast Asia than the West had Christian missionaries in the entire world! They were fighting a battle for men's minds and souls, and the United States was still relying on guns and helicopters to win the victory. I had a set of press credentials as a war correspondent in Vietnam, so that I could move freely around the country. (Don't ask how I got them; a few secrets must be kept!) In the early days of the war, I attended a press conference and heard an American general declare confidently, "There is *no* situation which we cannot handle. Everything is under control." How badly that general miscalculated! How little he understood the spiritual nature of the battle he was fighting! It did not surprise me a few years later that Vietnam fell, or Laos, or Cambodia. The Revolution arrived there long before the American soldiers did, and they were beaten before they began, in the battle that ultimately counted the most—the battle for the minds of the people. I could see the Revolution spreading.

We stepped up our activity in China and Vietnam. I visited every country which borders China. We are now in the process of printing Chinese Scriptures in India. If we send Bibles, already printed, into India, they are often destroyed, so we print them there, and teams drive them to the Chinese border in jeeps. The work in China is slow and hazardous. We had only eighteen trips into China all last year. The country is much less accessible than those in Eastern Europe, and places to cross the border by automobile or train are few and far between. The teams that make it in, however, report a great hunger for the Scripture, and a tremendous response to their efforts to discuss religion. There is definitely a large, virile church in China today, but it is suffering under a regime far more ruthless than those in Eastern Europe.

When Saigon fell to the North Vietnamese in 1975, and the Communists overwhelmed Cambodia and Laos to add those countries to their string, the Revolution once again shifted its sights to a new target. Eastern Europe is enslaved. Southeast Asia has now fallen. And the next battleground began to emerge. *Africa!* Of course! It had to be! The obvious target was Africa, with all its turmoil and bloodshed and political instability. Castro and Podgorny came in 1977 to add fuel to the smouldering—and already partly burning—conflict. Chou En-lai visited East Africa a few years ago and returned to Peking to declare publicly: "Africa is ripe for revolution!"

And so it is. But it is also ripe for revival—Christian revival. Africa is up for grabs, and the battle is on.

3

Black and White

Sometimes, God does His work in the most unlikely places!

He first pointed me toward Africa in a Baptist church in the Bulgarian city of Sofia. I ministered there on one of my Eastern European trips many years ago, and a handsome young black man made his way to the front of the building to talk with me after the service. It was something of a shock to see a black face in that part of the world, and I must have registered my surprise as I greeted him.

He was from Mozambique, he explained, and had been brought to Sofia by the Bulgarian government for free academic training. There were thousands more like him, he told me, young people from all across Africa, studying at Eastern European universities at the expense of the Communist regimes there. He himself was a Christian believer, but the offer of free college training had been too good to refuse, and now he was trapped in Bulgaria, unable to get back home until he had finished his studies. He had heard of my work among the Christians in Sofia, he said, and had come to meet me and give me a message:

"Brother Andrew," he told me solemnly, "the Revolution

is coming to my country. My father is the vice-president of FRELIMO (the Mozambican revolutionary movement), and the movement is small now, but it is growing. Andrew, after we have had our revolution, after we have closed the churches, killed the pastors, thrown all the Christians in prison, and thrown out all the missionaries, after we have done away with all the old Christianity—will you come and preach the true message of Jesus in our country?"

That sounded absurd! That was twenty years ago, and Mozambique was a seemingly stable Portuguese colony with a large, strong army. I had never heard of FRELIMO, or of any revolutionary movement in Mozambique at all. Yet here was a young black Christian telling me, here in a Bulgarian church, that the Revolution was coming to Africa!

(Eighteen years later, in 1975, FRELIMO drove out the last of the Portuguese army from Mozambique, took control of the government, and, true to the young man's prediction, began a harsh repression of the Christian church.)

Black Students in Europe

As I traveled through Europe in the years which followed that unusual encounter, I reflected on it frequently. Here we are, I thought, busily trying to get through to Christians behind Europe's Iron Curtain, and already the Revolution is at work in Africa, preparing for the day when that, too, will become a spiritual battleground. I began to meet other black students in university towns all across Eastern Europe. I talked with them, and the message was the same: "Do something *now* in Africa, while there is still time, before the doors are closed." I met them in Leipzig, in Prague, in Moscow, in Budapest. It is easy to meet black students in Eastern

Europe. They are usually lonely, separated from their own environment, often the object of discrimination in the towns where they are studying, eager to speak English with a friendly stranger. One sees them in restaurants or parks near the universities. I met many of them that way, and we talked.

It was an experience that opened my eyes. "What is happening in the world?" I asked myself. "And why do we Christians not know about it? Here are all these African students, thousands of young people training for Revolution in Africa, and we spend all our time in one small European portion of the world!" Gradually I developed a global view of the Revolution. I could see how it was spreading from Europe to Asia and then to Africa.

South African Potential

A few years later, I was asked to come to South Africa to speak to the Christians there about the needs of the suffering church. On this trip the Lord opened my eyes further to the potential of the African continent. He was dealing with me already about the need for a ministry to the black nations which were facing the Revolution. But before God could use me there, He had to show me the other side of the coin; He had to show me the great potential of the South African church and the role it can play in the spiritual battle for Africa.

I went to South Africa, I must confess, with a bit of a negative bias. I had been exposed to the Dutch press and all that has been written about white South Africans, and had developed a rather lofty lack of sympathy for them. I had rather accepted the popular view that they were intruders in the black man's continent, and that they should get out. I traveled to South Africa for the first time with little hope that the church there could be an effective force in the battle for African minds. What I found changed my mind. Although I may not be comfortable with their politics, I have had to swallow some of my preconceived biases against the South Africans, and recognize that they are a critical key to the spread of the Gospel on their continent.

I saw things that completely surprised me. I found in the South African people—black and white alike—a reverence for the Word of God, an openness to speak of Jesus, an eagerness to pray together and to witness, that is remarkably rare anywhere in the world. Everywhere I traveled, I found a genuine love for Jesus Christ, and a willingness to spend time and effort for the Kingdom. I urged young people to offer themselves for Christian service, and within three weeks saw five thousand young South Africans come forward in stadiums, schools, and churches to make that commitment. In my messages, I made the appeal tough, trying to screen out those who were not really determined. Sometimes, when hundreds of young people stood in commitment, I made them sit down, and made a tougher appeal. The harder I made it, the more young people stood. A school of evangelism, which still operates today, was started from those meetings.

The dedication which I found was not limited to the white church. I went into Soweto (a huge black population center) to hold meetings, and there told the story of the suffering church. I took an offering for the suffering churches of Europe, and watched in amazement as thousands of coins were placed into the hats that were passed. It was a beautiful sight—one group of Christians pouring out their love for another group of a different color and culture, in a gesture of Christian brotherhood. In Durban, a young Indian servant knocked on my hotel room door and told me the Holy Spirit had led him to pray for me. He laid hands on me then and there, and I felt a great anointing of the Holy Spirit. The next morning a black waiter in a restaurant stopped me to witness to me. He told me a great story of how the Lord had healed his mother-in-law, and we rejoiced there together!

It seemed that God was saying to me, "You must love *all* of Africa, not just black Africa. You must seek a way to harness the great potential of South Africa to reach the rest of Africa. The solution to the African crisis must have room for white Africans as well as black Africans, working side by side to win the battle against the Revolution." He was challenging me to stop looking at the African situation from a pro-South Africa or anti-South Africa perspective, and simply to trust God to use all African Christians to stem the revolutionary tide.

I came to see that here was a field God could use to get the message across to all of Africa. If South Africa would look to black Africa not as its problem, but as its opportunity, God could use its enormous spiritual and material resources to win the entire continent.

In the last meeting of that trip, I spoke in a tennis stadium, Ellis Park, in Johannesburg. As the service concluded a dignified white minister caught my attention. He was Koos Driescher, a well-known Dutch Reformed pastor. He told me he was at the point of retirement from his church, and felt moved to offer himself to spend the rest of his life in the ministry to the suffering church. I thought, "What do we do with an old man?" But I felt that it was of God, and he became a full-time worker for Open Doors in

Africa. He turned out to be so young at heart, and fresh in the Spirit, that he seems a young man to us now!

North Into Africa

As I traveled in other countries, I saw striking contrasts to the wealth and industrialized advancement of South Africa. From Johannesburg to the small countries of Central and East Africa is an enormous cultural leap. But one theme remained constant, wherever in Africa I have traveled: in Christ there is no black or white, no racial barriers. I also saw that the true church in Africa is a church of love and devotion, but still a church that badly needs help to withstand the Revolution. The Gospel is no less powerful there than anywhere else in the world, but there are awesome obstacles in the path of the church in almost every African country.

I preached in Malawi and Tanzania, in Kenya and Ethiopia. Everywhere there was a hunger for the Word, and everywhere the Africans who heard me seemed to identify easily with the message of the suffering church. There was a sense of the rapidly gathering storm, of the persecutions to come, a feeling that Africa could be next, that the tales of European and Asian suffering might be told increasingly of African believers in years to come. I spoke one day at a Christian youth camp in Southern Rwanda. It is one of the poorest countries in the world, with an actual average income of $17 per year per person. (For comparison: in the United States, the amount of gross national product per citizen is $7,060; in Rwanda, the figure is only $90.) I was there during a terrible economic crisis. Rwanda's fuel supply comes from Kenya through Uganda, and the Ugandan army had confiscated all of Rwanda's fuel, so the country was suffering with tremendous shortages of everything, even by its own standards.

But I told the story that day of Georgi Vins, a Russian pastor who is in prison, and those young people took an offering and asked me to get it into Russia somehow to Georgi Vins's family. That made me cry. It broke my heart. It was such a powerful example of one member of the body of Christ ministering to another member which suffers: poverty-stricken black Rwandans giving spontaneously to a suffering white brother in Russia! No regard for politics or color or nationality. That is the message for Africa; that is the spirit of Christ that is strong enough to stop the Revolution!

In Kenya, the university where I spoke was so overcrowded that people stood outside as far as they could hear. In Ethiopia, likewise, with people sitting on windowsills, the floor, everywhere. I emphasize this response to my message not to indicate that I drew a big crowd. Certainly there is nothing unusual about that in Africa. But the point is that I was preaching the message of the suffering church, warning that persecution is coming to Africa as it has to Asia, and the response from Christians I have talked to all over Africa is, "Yes, we know it is coming. We can feel the storm building. And we want to get ready for it." Africans have come to me in other parts of the world and said, "Brother Andrew, you have no idea how little time is left to do something in Africa." They feel uneasy about their safety, their families, their continent's future.

So our ministry began in Africa. It is my firm conviction that God wants Christians in Africa to prepare for whatever comes, to build the kind of church that can survive the Revolution, wherever it erupts. The African church must be a church that is built on the Bible. It must not be merely a cultural church, a pale copy of the American church or the British church. It must be a church that throbs with its own vision of Christ, which issues from its own access to the printed Word of God. The most immediate challenge of the outside church is to help provide the African church with the Bible, so that God can speak through His Word to the peculiar situation of Africans. As late as 1970, over half of Africa's population did not have access to any portion of the Scripture in their own language! How can we expect a strong African church if we have not paid the price to get the Bible to Africans?

Only With the Bible

A truly indigenous church in any land depends on the Bible's being available there. Only with the Bible can Africans build their own Christian faith, not echoing white missionary concepts, but forging their own unique spiritual armor from the raw material of Scripture. The Bible requires no assistance to do its work. It needs no missionary, no pastor, no explanation. It is itself the best possible evangelist, because God knows better than any human author how Africans—or Asians or Russians or anyone else—will see Jesus Christ and the Kingdom. If we are successful in getting the Bible into all parts of Africa *before* the Revolution comes, the church can survive under any regime, even if all the missionaries are chased away and all the church buildings closed.

Joseph Korbel is a Salvation Army officer who was imprisoned in Czechoslovakia for his ministerial activities there. He tells the story that one afternoon, while he was in prison for preaching, his wife managed to smuggle a sandwich into his cell. He waited until late at night to open the small package, and found between the two pieces of bread a small New Testament. Korbel's cell mate was insane—a madman who could not even make human sounds—who had been put in the cell with Korbel in an attempt to break the Christian's spirit. When he received that smuggled Bible, Korbel began to read it to his insane cell mate, a little each day, and over the next few weeks watched in amazement as the man came to his senses. He was literally healed—and brought to salvation—purely by the power of the Word of God!

The Chinese and Russians seem to understand the value of the Bible more than we do, because they are so determined to stop it. They fight the Bible more than anything else and, more than anything else, the believers in those areas ask for the Scriptures. There is a special power in the Bible, and it is that power that is most critical for the African church. A group of Ugandan ministers told me in Kampala, "There has never been a greater hunger for the Bible in Uganda than now. The demand is increasing. Even the Russians and other Communist visitors here in Uganda come to us secretly to ask for Bibles. We have no printing paper to print new Bibles. We can't get enough Bibles from outside the country because it is against the law for us to have foreign currency, and Ugandan shillings are worthless. Can you help us get printing paper or Bibles for our people?"

Another Christian brother operates a bookstore in an African country where the flow of Christian literature has been shut off. "Christians come to me and say, 'Can you get me a Bible or a Christian book?' and I have to say that I can do nothing for them. They will say, 'I'll take *anything,* if you can get it for me.' It breaks my heart. There is such a longing for the Word of God, and we inside this country can do nothing to help them."

Why must we be in chains before we will love the Bible and appreciate it as God's great gift to us? When the American prisoners-of-war returned from the North Vietnamese prison camps, they reported that remembering verses from the Bible was one of the strongest bonds among them. One of their major projects was to construct a Bible from memory; anyone who could recall a Scripture passage contributed. It seems that man always turns to God's Word when he has nothing left.

Translations are, of course, a major problem on a continent where literally hundreds of languages are spoken. But a growing problem with Africa is that of getting the Bibles delivered into areas where political repression makes it dangerous and illegal to take them across the country's borders. What do we do then? What do we do when Christians in Africa need Bibles, but there is no legal way to get them to the people? *We must smuggle them in, of course!* We already are making contacts, setting up delivery systems inside countries which are falling into Revolutionary hands. It is our best opportunity to minister to those people after the borders are legally closed.

We must get the Bible into every part of Africa—by conventional means if possible—but by unconventional means when there is no other way.

Coincidence or Guidance?

I believe in the power of God to help those who are willing to defy godless governments for the sake of the Kingdom. I have seen too many miracles performed in the past twenty years to doubt that God approves of that kind of aggressive evangelism. Some people have heard me tell of miraculous things occurring at so many border crossings, and have chalked it all up to luck or coincidence. It reminds me of a story I heard about an American college professor who was ridiculing students who believed the account in 2 Kings 19:34 where the Syrians laid siege in Israel. God said: "I will defend this city, to save it, for mine own sake, and for my servant David's sake." Then, in the night, the Lord smote 185 thousand in the camp of the Assyrians, and the Israelites arose in the morning to find all those dead bodies.

The college professor called this a coincidence. A young man protested, saying it was God's delivering His people, God's guidance, and all that.

"Now listen," said the professor, "if you walk in a jungle and all of a sudden a lion begins to jump at you, and as he is flying through midair, a coconut drops from a tree and lands on the head of the lion and knocks him out so you can escape, would you call that coincidence or guidance?"

The student thought for a while, with everybody staring at him. Then he replied, "Well, I might call that coincidence. But if I walk in the jungle and all of a sudden 185 thousand lions jump at me and as they are in midair, ready to land on me, at that moment 185 thousand coconuts dropped on their heads, then I would not call that coincidence. I would call it guidance or God's mighty intervention!"

I think that student won his argument.

I tell people that if I take Bibles across a border once and something remarkable happens, you might call it a coincidence. But I have been doing that for eighteen years—full time—with all my teams, and always something happens that distracts the guards' attention, or just makes us think that they haven't even seen us or seen our load. You cannot possibly call that coincidence. It's God's miraculous guidance and intervention!

It is that power of God that gives us the critical edge in our battle for Africa—if we only have the resolve and the courage to put it to the test.

4

The Tragedy of This Great Continent

One day in Africa I had an experience which moved me so deeply that I will never forget it. It seemed to show in a single moment all the pieces of the tragic African puzzle.

I was allowed to preach in a prison in a small country in Africa. It is a poor nation, and the scene of constant tribal warfare between the Hutus and the Tutsis. The government is a near-dictatorship, with few civil liberties. There are tens of thousands of refugees, and the prisons are overcrowded, with many political prisoners among those packed into the crude jails.

This particular prison was an ugly, square building out in the middle of nowhere, high walls, a heavy rusted iron gate to get in. Not a single window anywhere. All prisons are depressing, but this one was especially so. It seemed the kind of place that one never leaves after that iron gate slams shut behind him. I met the prison chaplain, an old man who lived in the village nearby, an alcoholic who was not a believer.

Inside the walls, the place was simply a square building divided into four separate areas, huge open rooms. In each there were packed hundreds of prisoners, who slept side by side on the floor. To one side was a single toilet area, overflowing with dirty toilet water and bad smells. The floor of the place was dirty, and most of the time—including this time—it stayed muddy. All the prisoners were invited to assemble in one of these four areas for a religious service, and they crowded together, hundreds of them, standing barefooted in the mud, filling even the toilet area. We had our backs against one wall, standing on a metal box to keep our feet dry. Everything was so bleak in that place, so terribly depressing! It was a moving experience to me as I looked at those men, because I knew that so many of them were political prisoners, and not common criminals, by any means.

As I looked at them, I saw really beautiful people. The Lord gave me a tremendous compassion for them. Lots of them were young men who were simply on the wrong side of the regime, and were shut up in this horrible place. I poured out my heart to them, explained what it meant to be a Christian, to have this Man Jesus come into your life and change everything. When I finished, I was at first reluctant to give an invitation, but felt that I should do so anyway. I had spoken for over an hour, and those men had stood in the mud and listened quietly. No one moved at all. They listened to what I said and took it all in like a dry sponge soaks up water.

"I can't promise you freedom from this prison," I said finally, "but I can promise you a spiritual freedom in Jesus Christ. Which of you men would want this new life in Jesus?" There was a man standing on my right, an elderly gentleman with curly gray hair. He looked at me with big, sincere eyes and said, "Sir, *all* of us would want to follow such a Man, this Jesus that you speak about." When I repeated that to the crowd, and asked, "Is it true that you want more of this Jesus?" Hundreds of heads nodded emphatically back at me. Again I sought to explain more clearly what it was all about. I explained the need for a break with sin in their personal lives. Still they insisted they wanted this Jesus.

So we prayed together, and I tried to introduce them to Jesus. When I opened my eyes, there were many tears in that place, in eyes and on cheeks. I too was crying. I felt so very bad because I knew that outside that building there was a little Volkswagen to take me away from this horrible, infested place. In it was a thermos of hot coffee. I would drive away and drink my coffee and live in totally different surroundings. And I would have to leave those men (whom I called my brethren in Christ) with no Bibles and no freedom. I stayed the rest of the afternoon with them, singing hymns and telling Bible stories. Finally the time came to leave, and I left with a heavy heart and slow steps.

The Bad and the Ugly

As I drove away from the prison, I thought how clearly that experience includes all that is bad and ugly about the Africa of today. There is the crushing poverty and disease. There is the political upheaval that fills prisons with men whose only crime is to say the wrong word, or belong to the wrong tribe, or church, or political party. There is the harsh, sinful treatment of man toward his brother. There is the isolation from the eyes and concern of the outside world, including the Christian world. And there is the impotence of the church, represented by a single, unregenerated chaplain who has no Bibles, no Christian love, and no born-again witness for those men who need it so desperately.

Most of Africa's 400 million people are not behind bars, but most of them in one way or another suffer from the forces that created that unspeakable African prison.

What are these forces?

POVERTY. To describe the poverty of Africa, it is not enough simply to say that the annual per capita income—for the entire continent—is one hundred and fifty dollars, compared, for example, to thirty-five hundred dollars in the United States. The situation is more desperate than even that grim statistic reveals. Eighteen of the world's twenty-eight poorest countries are in sub-Saharan Africa (the part of Africa south of the Sahara desert). Only 17 percent of the people can read or write. Out of every hundred infants born, fifteen die before their first birthday. The average life span in Africa is *thirty years less* than in the United States!

TRIBALISM. Tribalism is a fact of life in Africa. It produces constant fighting and makes refugees of hundreds of thousands of Africans. The United Nation's High Commission for Refugees reported last year that more than a million Africans are on the run, in exile from their home countries. In Burundi, the Hutu and Tutsi tribes engage in programs of genocide in their conflict with one another, killing tens of thousands of innocent villagers and sending more into flight. In Southern Sudan, bitter fighting between black tribesmen and Arabs has gone on for years, with an estimated 180 thousand Sudanese now living in exile in nearby countries. Some forty thousand Congolese who fled that country during fighting in the Katanga province still live in poverty outside Zaire. And the list goes on and on. "Many

African refugees," says the November 8, 1976, *U.S. News and World Report,* "live in constant fear, knowing that relatives and friends have been jailed, tortured or slain. Few harbor hopes of returning home soon."

NATIONALISM AND POLITICAL UPHEAVAL. These are forces which have made Africa a place of continuing turmoil. Africa was for many years a collection of colonies, ruled and exploited by European powers. But since World War II there has been a change in that. A worldwide wave of nationalism has led dozens of African countries to gain independence from outside powers, and with independence have come intense military struggles for leadership. The withdrawal of colonial powers left a political vacuum in many countries, and the common people have been major casualties of the resultant instability. While many of the white colonial powers were indeed oppressive, the shift to nationalistic government has not solved that problem.

A small black elite has taken over in many areas. A few years ago the poor black man was carrying the white man on his back. Now he is carrying a black man on his back. Even with liberation from colonialism, the suffering and discontent of the typical African continue to smolder. The problems remain the same: the poverty is the same, the cruelty is the same, the senseless killing is the same.

DISCRIMINATION. The white colonial governments in Africa have been an easy target for many years, and many black Africans are pointing out that discrimination still exists, and still is at the root of many of the continent's ills.

"This is not discrimination by bloody white settlers or colonialists against Africans," one nationalist leader wrote recently, "but discrimination by Africans against Africans; discrimination by the 'black suit' townsmen; discrimination by the educated men in power against their fellow countrymen—their brothers and sisters, mothers and fathers, against their own folk in the village. African leaders, you who fought so bravely against colonialism—you who preach humanism and African socialism—you stand idly by while your educated colleagues carry out such ruthless exploitation among your weaker subjects!"

Breeding Ground for Revolution

It is into this setting of poverty, violence, and uncertainty that the Revolution has come. The perfect breeding ground for the Revolution is man at war—man at war with himself, with society, with other races, with labor conditions, with religious conflicts, with poverty and injustice. Never in history has there been a place and a time more ripe for Revolution than the Africa of today.

What Is Revolution?

By *Revolution*, I mean the worldwide pressure to destroy the church as an effective witness to men and women. The Revolution is a violent, determined response to the problems of mankind that offers a godless alternative. It says, "Christianity and its ideas have been around for all these years, and look what a mess we have." The alternative it offers is a new world order based on a denial of God as an outmoded myth. The Revolution is a movement to capture men's minds and convince them that the problems of the world can only be solved by destroying the church with all its values and teachings. The Revolution preaches that violence is an acceptable method of gaining power, that individual human beings are dispensable—if their deaths will aid the movement.

Is the Revolution then the same as communism? one might ask. No, it is not necessarily communistic, though it might be and often is. Certainly worldwide communism is part of the Revolution, even the greatest part of it. But the Revolution has many other faces. In a particular case, it may not take the form of communism at all. It may take the expression of nationalism in a given country, or of existential philosophy on a university campus, or of many other things. But its effect is always the same: to destroy the church—whether through force of arms, or intellectual arguments, or social ridicule—and to tear people away from the values of the true God, so that they have no source of authority but the Revolution itself.

In the Revolution, hatred finds an outlet to destroy the church. The Revolution seeks to change men by pointing out to them their miseries, then blaming everything on Christianity and all that is associated with it. So men join the Revolution, seeking a new world at whatever cost in blood and suffering. It was in Havana, Cuba, that I once saw a quotation from Che Guevara emblazoned on the wall of a hospital: "If this Revolution is not aimed at changing people, then I am not interested." *That* is the power of the Revolution—to change men by winning their minds.

It is important to remember that this Revolution will not always operate under the name of communism *per se*. This is particularly true in Africa, where it often takes the form of black nationalism or anti-imperialism. A ruler such as Idi Amin in Uganda would stoutly insist that he is not a Communist, that he seeks only an independent course for his country. And it is probably true that Amin's loyalty lies not with Moscow, but with himself and his tribe only—at least for the time being. But his ruthless campaign against the church puts him squarely in the front lines of the Revolution nevertheless.

The nature of the Revolution is essentially ideological. It is not political or military—those are only the weapons that it uses. And because it is a spiritual movement at its root, it must be fought with spiritual weapons. America and the West have sought too long to oppose the spread of communism with conventional military means. This approach never works. When the opposing cause is an ideological one, the more one kills of the enemy, the more martyrs one provides for their cause. That is exactly what they want. We should have learned that lesson from the sad experience of the Americans in Vietnam. The Americans had all the military might, but the Revolution had won the ideological war before the fighting even began. The fall of Saigon was only a matter of time.

It Can Happen Here

Too often we of the Western world think we can win by spending enough money. We think that we can buy friends, that we can build our system on weapons and technology alone. But the thing we need most in Africa is for more Christians to have a personal sense of urgency about the battle for that continent, and a *strategic* view of the battle, that is, a recognition of it as a spiritual struggle. But we have no sense of reality. No sense of strategy. No sense of timing. We are fighting professional revolutionaries who work strategically. They are not panicked by failure or lulled to sleep by success. We must somehow develop that same sense of strategy that they have.

I have a young missionary friend, now a colleague of mine in Open Doors, who served for several years in Vietnam. He was at a conference of Christians in Da Nang shortly before it fell to the Communist armies. He told me that on that very day the Vietnamese pastors had spent the session discussing their "Ten Year Plan" for Vietnam. It was business-as-usual—plans and projections—just as if the world were not exploding outside! They didn't have ten years. They didn't have even ten days! But they seemed oblivious to it. They vastly underestimated the power of the Revolution, and while they should have been preparing the church to live under persecution, too many of them were talking about what buildings they would erect in the 1980s!

There are two things I have heard all over the world when I talk about the Revolution. *One:* It will never happen here. *Two:* We *thought* it would never happen here. There seems to be nothing else. In so many countries in Africa, I have heard it over and over: *It will never happen here.* And the countries of Eastern Europe, where the freedoms have been crushed by the Russian revolutionaries, and in Asia where the Chinese-armed troops have enslaved Vietnam, Laos, and Cambodia, the line has only a single sad difference: We *thought* it would never happen here.

The flow of history can still be interrupted in Africa. Only a few countries are already Marxist, and the leaders even there do not have a strong ideological hold on the mass of people, only a military one. Our greatest weapon is people with changed hearts, hearts which have been changed by the love of Christ.

U.S. Secretary of State Henry Kissinger (not a man given to overstatement) said last year in an unpublished speech that "never before in history has so revolutionary a reversal occurred with such rapidity" as the rise of black nationalism in Africa. Fifteen years ago, British Prime Minister Harold Macmillan reviewed the state of African affairs and proclaimed: "The wind of change is blowing through the continent." That wind has by now become a gale—a hurricane—that threatens to blow the church right off the African map.

5

Healing Bodies and Losing Souls

Most of us grew up hearing tales of fearless white missionaries, in British khaki shorts and pith helmets, taking the Gospel to Deepest Dark Africa. We have all heard the story of that adventurous reporter named Henry Stanley pushing through the bush to speak those memorable lines, "Doctor Livingstone, I presume . . ." when he finally reached the famous missionary. To most people in the Christian world, it seems that the word *Africa* almost automatically evokes the word *missionary,* so frequently have the two been associated in the literature and historical lore of the church.

And it is true. Africa is the most familiar mission field in the world. Over the past hundred years it has had the attention of more foreign missionaries than any other single area. It is a great irony that this missionary-saturated continent should be the part of the world most completely vulnerable to an anti-Christian Revolution!

Perhaps *irony* is too gentle a word. It is more than that; it is a tragedy, a tragedy of monumental proportions. And it deserves an attempt at explanation. How is it possible for a Christian church that has seemed so well entrenched to be now so vulnerable to the "winds of change"? Is it possible that, with all its missions appeals and millions of dollars, the church has failed in Africa in these hundred-plus years?

The painful answer is *yes*.

There are many ways in which the Christian church has made valuable contributions to African life: Hundreds of schools, hospitals, orphanages, and churches exist which otherwise would not be there. In 1957 Adlai Stevenson, the American statesman, visited Africa, and the thing that most amazed him was the graves of the missionaries: "Anyone who travels in Africa is constantly reminded of missionaries' heroism," he said. "They laid a groundwork in religion, health, and education under difficult and dangerous circumstances. What they have done is almost beyond belief. They fought yellow fever, dysentery, parasites. And the gravestones I saw! Their gravestones—all through Africa!"

Thousands of individual Africans owe their personal knowledge of Christ to Western missionaries. Christian missionaries have gone there for a hundred years, and they have been loving and dedicated to their work, leaving the continent salted with their own graves as testimony to their sincerity. But somehow their sincerity has not been enough to immunize the African nations against the spread of the Revolution.

The Tragic Failure of the Church

The Revolution always thrives on the failure of the church. It is tempting to say that the rising wave of Revolution has caused the church to fail in Africa. Actually, the reverse is true. The Revolution is succeeding *because* of the failure of the church. Whenever the church fails, the Revolution must succeed. They are two sides of a coin. If the spiritual hunger of man is not satisfied by the church, it leaves a vacuum into which the poison of the Revolution will inevitably flow. The great Russian writer Solzhenitsyn, discussing the Bolshevik Revolution in Russia in 1917, said: "The truth requires me to state that the condition of the Russian church at the beginning of the Twentieth Century is one of the principal *causes* for the inevitability of the Revolutionary events" (from *Solzhenitsyn's Religion* by Niels C. Nielsen, Jr.).

I have been in the Kremlin museum in Moscow, and seen a hint of what he is talking about. Displayed there is a huge Bible used by the Czars. It is covered with gold, with diamonds and jewels on the lid so heavy, it can hardly be opened with one hand. The robes of the patriarchs were embroidered with twenty kilos of gold and silver thread. And where did all this wasteful wealth come from? From the poor peasant people—who were lucky to have bread to eat. The church in Russia sucked their blood and never gave them the gospel of love in return. The church left the streets and retired to the cathedrals. It became an arm of the established powers, and not an evangelistic force with a cup of cool water and the Gospel of salvation. So the Revolution came to Russia.

In Africa the church has in a certain sense also fallen short, though in a different way, and so the Revolution is also at its doorstep. We have Christianized the African continent without giving enough of the people a first-person faith. Too many missions have responded to the physical suffering of the people and stopped there. We have built hospitals and schools and somehow lost the focus on the spiritual needs of the people. It is good to feed the hungry and educate the ignorant and doctor the sick—but if we do all that for a man and do not present him the message of a Jesus who makes him a new, born-again creature, we have failed. We have ministered to the body only, when the soul, too, is sick. We have only produced a healthier, better-educated African, whose heart is still empty. And he will find something in the passionate ideology of the Revolution to fill that empty heart.

The Communists understand this principle better than we do. They have not planted orphanages in Africa, as the church has. They are after the minds of the people, and that is the constant focus of their work. Forget about the African's poverty and disease and human misery, they say; just give him something to hate, and he will be a revolutionary who ignores all his privations for the cause. We must spend our effort giving him something to love, and someone who loves him—then join hands with him to help him solve his other problems.

The Cultural Trap

The first and most basic problem of our missions effort in Africa is that we have presented a Christian message which is inseparably bound to our own Western way of life. Too many missions have gone to Africa more in the service of their Western culture, and even of their particular Western governments, than working directly in the service of the particular tribe or group to whom they minister. Every missionary should have two homelands: heaven and the country he works in. That leaves out the country he comes from. That attitude must somehow be the starting point of every missionary's work.

Unfortunately, too many Africans have come to see Christianity as an English or European or American faith. A black African writer named Erasto Muga says, "The important thing to remember is that the white missionaries in East Africa failed to distinguish themselves in the African eye from the colonial authorities. This made Africans rebel against Christianity and its teachings." We have gone into Africa to build an Anglicized church, and when the Africans reject our culture, it is unavoidable that they also reject our God.

A black African writer describes a typical missions effort in this biting sketch:

> The child comes to the church school dressed in his front-kerchief and bared buttocks, and squats before a nun or a man dressed in a suit. During the music lesson he is taught to sing:
>
> Baa baa black sheep
> Have you any wool?
> Yes, sir, yes, sir,
> Three bags full—
> One for the Master,
> One for the Dame,
> And one for the little boy
> Who lives down the lane.
>
> He must wonder what this song is all about! Sheep in his village are reared for eating, for the sacrifice when woman has broken a taboo, and for payment of bridal wealth; and they do not have bags of wool! The master—that must be the class teacher, but what does he want a bag of wool for? And the

> dame? Is this the old grandmother? And the little boy, his playmate, does not play with a bag of wool! So he probably does not think about the song at all, repeating it meaninglessly as he repeats the other meaningless songs and chants in the church. Later he reads strange stories about a white boy named Jack and a white girl named Jill going up the hill. On Sunday morning they go to church and sing songs about a white man Jesus. And when you sing you stand stiff, and you do not look around you. You must not appear to be enjoying it. There are no drums in the church, and the tunes are so dull! [From the Bulletin of the Africa Institute of South Africa.]

What God wants is an *African* church, and tying the claims of Christ to the Western culture surely dooms the whole project to failure. We make the Christian faith too easy a target that way. The revolutionaries say, "Look, Christianity has been here all this time. What have the Christians done for you? They put you in slave ships—owned by Dutch Calvinists—and sold you as slaves in America, the most Christian nation in the world!" Christians are an easy target in Africa, an easy scapegoat. But because of the sins and mistakes of our forefathers, we cannot just give it up. We must be willing to say, "Christianity has nothing to do with my country or your country or anyone else's. It is for individuals." Only that way can we get a fresh start—not just by saying that, but by *showing* it.

Tying our faith to our culture puts us at an extra disadvantage in Africa, where our major rivals in evangelism have always been the Muslims. Islam has been seeking converts in Africa for over a hundred years too, and their culture is much more compatible with African culture than Christianity is. Swahili, the widespread language of many natives, is in fact a fusion of the Bantu language with Arabic, developing from the intermarriage of Arab traders and Bantu natives in East Africa in the last century. Africans have far less to abandon culturally by converting to Islam than to Christianity, and that religion is growing rapidly in Africa.

Christian Racism

A second major weakness of the Christian effort has been the constantly recurring evidence of racism by the church itself. That is a tough criticism to accept, but honesty requires us to take a hard look at ourselves and our racial attitudes. We have preached that in Christ all men are one, but frequently have practiced a different thing entirely.

Historically, the entire Protestant missionary movement in Africa began from a racist base. Although the Moravian missionary Count Zinzendorf never went to Africa, he did go to African slaves in the West Indies. In 1731, he paid a call to King Christian VI of Denmark, his personal friend. The king, though himself a devout Lutheran, was outraged when told that his friend would be preaching to black people.

"How can you do that? They are the firewood of hell! It is impossible for a black person ever to go to heaven. What a fool you are!"

Count Zinzendorf interrupted him, and calmly replied, "There is only one way for either you or a black slave to get to heaven, and that is through the blood of Jesus Christ." The king was so angry that he almost had him arrested and thrown into prison!

> Do you really believe [the king said] that it could be in the purpose of God that Negro slaves can be saved and go to heaven? You cannot possibly mean to say that with God there is no difference between race and color and that a black man is worth just as much with God as his white master? Yes, that there would in heaven be no difference between a slave and his master? You do admit, don't you, that God has indeed cursed Negroes and left them to their own to be doomed for time and eternity? How else could slavery be possible, how could God allow that we steal these people or (shall I say) creatures and exploit them for our own use? Don't you feel that by preaching to these creatures that God loves them and that He wants to redeem them and wants them in heaven that you condemn the entire white race and you insult them. Because, either you're right and slavery is from Satan and all those who are engaged in it are servants of Satan, or they are really cursed, but then you have no right to intervene and preach a false Gospel to them. You would be creating a terrible disaster in that way.

These are the actual words of King Christian VI of Denmark in 1731. This was the prevailing theology and philosophy at the time of the birth of the Protestant missionary movement; and it was also the time of the colonizing powers; it was about the same time the Dutch set foot on the southern tip of Africa.

The prevailing theology was that the black man had no soul. That was during the time that colonizing began, the slave trade flourished, and the Western culture first showed its hand in Africa. Since then, the level of sophistication has risen greatly, but the basic inability to see the black man as a fully equal human being remained. When the missionary flood began in the early twentieth century, many enthusiastic Christians rushed to the conclusion that Africans could not conceive of God. One, after spending ten months in Nigeria, wrote of the people among whom he ministered: "The people are of a low type. They live for the most part in crude nudity. The older men and women can recall the taste of human flesh. They are all lazy. They do not know God."

Racism has compromised the effectiveness of the church in Africa, and does still today. The issue is one of human dignity, of treating black men as men, not as children or primitives. We have patronized and babied the African people too long—long after they have become full partners in the work of Kingdom. It is an ingrained posture of superiority that has become a part of the unconscious style of many missionaries, and it insults and reduces the very people whom they seek to win. W. E. Owen, a veteran European missionary in Kenya, describes the problem this way:

> Nothing alienates the African sentiment more than injustice; and the hasty, cutting words, the quick blow, or maybe even the impetuous kick, once given, as alas it has been given only too frequently, harm the missionary in the eyes of the Africans. Africans see that Europeans do not use each other so, and have sense enough to see that he is treated differently. There is something very sad

> when Africans say of a missionary: "He does not regard us as human beings."

The church must restore the sense of dignity to man; and, when we do that, the Revolution cannot get an easy grip on him.

The Leadership Gap

Perhaps our greatest shortcoming in Africa has been our failure to develop leadership among native Christians. This, more than any other lack, haunts us now, as missionaries are being driven from country after country, and the wave of nationalism makes white foreigners none too welcome in many others. There were only three independent nations south of the Sahara when World War II ended; today there are more than forty of them! Whether by violence or by political order, the missionaries are pulling out of Africa, leaving the church in the hands of local Christians who have not been trained for the job.

The secretary-general of the Uganda Bible Society told me last year: "In the past, missionaries did almost everything for us. We never knew what they did or how they did it. They didn't have bad intentions; they just thought they would always be here to run things. When they had to leave, we had to take over, and we are not ready. All Ugandan churches are now led by Ugandans. Though the church is one hundred years old, we are terribly young in leadership." And it is true. Many church leaders in that country had so much done for them by foreigners that they have been overwhelmed by the recent changes, simply caught in the flow of events for which we had not prepared them.

One of the most dedicated young missionaries I know is

John Kearn, who served for eight years in Laos. He now works with Open Doors in Africa, and he looks back on his ministry in Laos with one major regret. "We always thought we had more time," he told me recently. "We never created leadership. We kept things to ourselves too long, just didn't give the church over to the people in time. We always made the big decisions, and even when we asked for their opinions, we usually had our minds already made up. That was our big mistake. When God starts a church, He has the leaders in that church. We must simply recognize them and be willing to give things over to them. We failed to teach them to get along without us. We failed to make ourselves unnecessary—that was our biggest mistake!"

John Kearn left Laos after eight years, and soon afterward that country fell to the Communists. It is unlikely that Western missionaries will be able to return there in the near future. The lesson of Laos for Africa is clear: the indigenous church must be built today, because in the rapidly changing continent of Africa, there may well be no tomorrow.

The Other Side

Why is it constructive to acknowledge the areas in which the church has failed in Africa?

Because there is a dominant sense of defeat and fatalism among many Christians who look at the onrushing Revolution in that continent. They look at the collapse of the missionary effort in so many countries and feel that somehow the Gospel just cannot save Africa from the Revolution. The church has been tried in Africa, they say, and it didn't work. So we just throw up our hands and accept the victory of the Revolution as something we cannot stop. *But that is not true.*

It has been said before, and it is truer of Africa than anywhere: The problem is not that the Gospel has been tried and found wanting; the problem is that the Gospel has *not been tried.*

The Gospel changes the hearts of men, and when their hearts are changed, their minds are changed; and when their minds are changed, the Revolution is beaten! No political deals, no modern weapons, no guerrilla army, no human force can win the victory for the Revolution if the sheer, unadorned, un-Americanized, color-blind Gospel of Jesus Christ has touched and won the hearts of enough of the people! More important than all the social, medical, educational, and humanitarian programs is the simple act of putting the Bible into a man's hand so that God can speak to him through it. More important than all the political lectures and appeals is the task of telling him the story of Jesus and His death and Resurrection. That sounds so simple, but it is just simple enough to work! Those are the basics of the Great Commission that we must get back to! If we do, it is not too late to save Africa.

Festo Kivengere, the well-known Ugandan minister, tells a story which so powerfully illustrates what I am saying:

> We were attending in Kenya a great meeting of some 11,000 people. Most of them were Christians, born-again men and women; but there were some who had come as spectators, or drawn by the Spirit to be saved. It was not long after the terrorism in Kenya when hundreds of African Christians died at the hands of the Mau Mau, witnessing for the Lord. They had died gloriously: some of them were just girls, some were young men and women, some

were older. And as the gospel was being preached in this great meeting, the Spirit of God was making people respond. People were weeping.

A man stood up, absolutely overcome. He was a tough fellow, a Kikuyu by tribe, a taxi-driver in the City of Nairobi: not the emotional type, but he was shaking from head to foot, weeping. He said, "I am much worse than a beast of a man. I have been a terrorist for the past three years: I have murdered more than sixty people. And yet somehow I feel the love of God has received me." He began to weep again, and all the poeple bowed their heads in prayer.

"I never expected God to receive me," he went on. "Now I know he has done so. But there is a woman in this crowd whose husband I helped to hang in the bedroom, in front of her. Can such a woman forgive such a beast of a man?"

And to be sure, she was there. She stood up and walked quietly from where she was, to where the man who murdered her husband was standing. Every head was bowed; no one knew what was going to happen. Then this woman stretched out her hand and put it in the hand of the man who murdered her husband, saying, "I forgave you that night, when my husband prayed for you. You are now my brother!"

That taxi-driver is now an evangelist. I have witnessed with him side by side—a wonderful experience. When he speaks about the love of God, he weeps: you can't blame him!

Could any of us devise skillful enough an argument to win such a man? Could we wipe from his heart the hatred that made him kill? Could we possibly reach inside his mind and convince him that his politics were evil? Of course not! If we rely on our own power alone, we would write him off as a hopeless enemy in the battle for Africa. But the Gospel of Christ changed his heart in a moment's time, and made him an ally of the church, an evangelist to others!

It is far too early to write off Africa. No need to grovel in our mistakes, to dwell on our failures. No need to throw up our hands in defeat. If God changed one man, He can change ten. If He changed ten, He can change ten thousand; He can change an entire continent!

6

The Legacy of Marx and Lenin

I have always distrusted those people who blame the Communists for everything!

That may seem a strange thing for me to say, since to many people I am a symbol of resistance to the Communist governments of Eastern Europe. But it is true, nevertheless; I find it amazing the great variety of ills that some westerners manage to trace to the influence of communism. I know people who see Communists lurking behind virtually all their troubles, from the prices of food in Paris to the failure of the corn crop in Kansas. A friend recently showed me an article in an American newspaper which declared that the change from Fahrenheit to Celsius in American thermometers is a diabolical Commie plot!

My very first trip to the United States, in fact, came at the invitation of an organization that was (unknown to me) totally obsessed with fighting communism. As I found when I got to their conference in a western state, these people had no idea what they were *for;* they only knew what they were *against*, and that was the Communists. They apparently thought, because of my reputation for smuggling Bibles behind the Iron Curtain, that I would give a red-hot speech condemning the Communists. When I declined to do so, they were very upset. So upset, in fact, that they dumped me right then and there, without even air fare to get home to Holland. I had to hole up in a hotel, with no money, until my wife could send me money to fly home. I had just enough money to buy a carton of yogurt each day, which I ate in my room, using the back of my toothbrush as a spoon! What an introduction to America!

David Adeney, an outstanding Christian leader in China who witnessed the takeover there by the Red Army, has said, "To paint communism in completely black colors and to fail to appreciate its very real achievements will only close the door to any meaningful communication of the Gospel." I agree with that, and I think it is not at all constructive to spend all one's time fighting communism as a political system *per se*. There are too many man-made systems which are cruel and evil to limit oneself to an attack on communism alone.

People somehow expect me to be a vehement anti-Communist, and I simply have never had the time nor the inclination to become a crusader against communism. I am not anti-Communist; I am pro-Christian. I am pro-people. God called me to take the Gospel to people, and whatever stands between them and me is my enemy.

But I must tell you that communism is hard at work in the Revolution in Africa. Moscow, Peking, and Havana all have their hands in the African pot right up to their elbows. The clearer we are on that critical point, the more clearly we can see what the stakes in the battle for Africa really are. The African crisis cannot be fully understood in detachment from the events in history which have led up to it. It is a part of a larger pattern of worldwide agitation and violence that is generated and inspired by the persistent fight of communism against the church. In a wide range of operations, the legacy of Marx and Lenin can be seen:

MILITARY TROOPS. As many as twelve thousand Cuban combat troops, fighting with arms provided by Russia, have won major military victories for the MLPA, the Angolan liberation movement which now controls most of that country. Cuban combat troops are known to be presently in Congo Brazzaville, Tanzania, Equatorial Guinea, Somalia, Guinea, Sierra Leone, South Yemen, and Mozambique. In addition, military advisors from Russia and China help train and lead the armies of at least a dozen other African nations where ground troops are not present.

ARMS AND FINANCIAL AID. The shipment of arms from Russia and China to developing African nations has reached enormous proportions. A CIA report, recently made public, showed that over nine thousand Soviet and Chinese military technicians and almost forty thousand economic advisors are "on loan" from those countries to African nations. This amounts to an almost staggering Communist presence in these countries, with most of this number coming from China. China also leads the way in economic aid, with 55 percent of her total foreign aid commitments in 1975 going to Africa.

PROPAGANDA. Communist books, leaflets, and magazines are much more readily available in some African countries than are Christian or Western-printed material. Thousands of full-time literature distributors are employed throughout the continent, putting cheap reading matter into the hands—and the languages—of the people. It is a frightening repeat of the old story: Christian mission schools teach the people how to read; the Communists give them material for reading. Other, larger projects are also part of the propaganda effort, such as a four-million-dollar shortwave broadcasting station which the Chinese built a few years ago outside Dar es Salaam (capital of Tanzania). It is equipped with a powerful 100-kilowatt transmitter for use in broadcasting propaganda into Mozambique, Rhodesia, and South Africa in vernacular African languages.

ACADEMIC TRAINING. Perhaps the most frightening evidence of the Communist presence in Africa is its policy of exporting African college students to foreign universities. One of these students, whom I met at Karl Marx University in Leipzig, East Germany, gave me a hint at the deceitful way many of them are recruited. He was about to graduate as a teenager from a mission school in South West Africa, and attended a meeting which was held by an East German recruiter. After the recruiter had spoken, extending an offer of free academic training as "guest" of the East German government, he offered to answer questions from the group. The first student raised his hand: "What about religious freedom in your country?" he asked. "We are all from Christian schools and wish to continue our religious activities."

"No problem," the recruiter lied. "We are a Christian nation. The Protestant church began in our country. You will have complete freedom of religion in Leipzig." Then, to further reassure the black students, he closed the meeting with prayer, effectively silencing any further questions about Christian liberty!

When the meeting was over, the young Christian student

told the recruiter, "Sir, your kind offer sounds very good. Please let me have two days to go home and talk it over with my family and my pastor."

"I'm very sorry," the recruiter answered. "But that will be impossible. We have no time for you to be indecisive. You must either leave tomorrow, or the offer is withdrawn. It is now or never."

The chance for free college training was so fantastic for this sincere young African that he took it. But when he got to East Germany, he had no freedom of religion, and no way to get out. He could get back to Africa only by paying his own air fare, and it was illegal for him as a resident foreigner to have dollars, so there he was. Trapped. I never knew when or how he got out.

I met a group of young men in Bulgaria who had been similarly recruited from Ghana. They arrived in Bulgaria and, at my invitation, began going to a Protestant church there, taking scores of fellow students with them. Then the authorities cracked down. "We brought you here to study, not to go to church," they said. When the students protested that they had been told they could worship, the university started scheduling required lectures on Sundays during church time. The students refused to attend. Then the university shut off all the heat in their dormitory rooms—it was during the cold Bulgarian winter—but still the students wouldn't budge. Finally the Communist authorities sent in a charter plane and shipped the leaders of the protest—seventy of them—back home to Ghana.

Russia hopes that giving African students free academic training will pay off for them, and indeed it is doing that. But it also gives many African students a glimpse of the Soviet "workers' paradise" that repels some students as it attracts others. There are constant reports of African students encountering the same racism and repression in Russia of which the Russians so vigorously accuse the West. On one occasion, seven hundred Ghanian students broke through police cordons and rushed to the gates of the Kremlin in a bitter demonstration protesting racial discrimination by Russian authorities. They carried placards reading STOP KILLING AFRICANS and RUSSIAN FRIENDSHIP with skull and crossbones underneath. In another incident, twenty-nine Kenyans returned from the University of Baku (Russia) with tales of cold, hunger, perpetual propaganda, and "unbearable discrimination."

When I met the first Mozambican student in Sofia so long ago, I had no idea on how large a scale the Russians and Chinese operated this program. Last year there were 14,895 black African students in universities in Communist countries—two-thirds of them in Russia—all at the expense of the Communists. An ominous note in the 1976 government report states: "Graduates of Communist universities are beginning to move into influential positions in their home countries, especially in Africa." Gradually, despite the protests and breakdowns here and there, the program is having its effect.

LIBERATION MOVEMENTS. No other type of Communist involvement in Africa has so immediate and violent an effect on the battle for Africa as does the support of liberation movements and revolutionary fronts in various countries. The strategy is a simple one: throw money, arms, and support to one side of small wars, wherever they break out, help that side win, and demand reciprocal "friendship" when that group is firmly in power. On a continent where so many natives have legitimately and passionately fought for their freedom in the past thirty years, there is a fertile field for Communist infiltration. The rhetoric of communism mingles easily with the slogans of national liberation. It is only after the war is over that the "freedom fighter" discovers that his revolutionary comrade—whether Russian or Chinese—is himself a greedy, harsh slave master.

In *Angola,* Russia and Cuba threw their support behind the MPLA, and that faction has virtually eliminated its opposition in the country, though it represents only about 20 percent of all Angolans.

In *South West Africa,* the liberation front is called SWAPO, and it too operates a constant guerrilla war, largely with Russian support.

Children in *Tanzania* come home from school singing a song they have been taught by nationalist teachers: "Kill your mother! Kill your father!" It is a hint of the breakdown of Tanzanian home life that has accompanied the pervasive Chinese influence in that country. Families are being forcibly moved into "resettlement areas" by the revolutionary government there, which has also brought tens of thousands of Chinese workers into the country.

In *Mozambique,* the Portuguese colonial regime was overwhelmed by the FRELIMO (Front for Liberation of Mozambique) revolutionary movement in 1975. FRELIMO began its fight twenty years ago with only two hundred and fifty men, against a well-equipped Portuguese army of forty thousand soldiers. Receiving constant infusions of money and arms from the Chinese and Russians, the movement eventually gained the support of the Mozambican masses, and moved from guerrilla warfare to outright control of the country.

There is nothing wrong with nationalism in itself. There

is nothing wrong with an Angolan or a Mozambican wishing his country to be governed by Angolans or Mozambicans rather than by Europeans in some remote capital. It is natural for a young black African to demand and strive for a nation that is governed by its own people. But too often in Africa it is not working out that way. Too often the Revolution has merely produced a change of slave masters, and not an elimination of slavery.

If a nationalistic revolution becomes an enemy of the church, if it cuts off a man's access to God, if it opposes the free exercise of Christian worship and witness, then it is evil and it must be fought! However much we are inclined to sympathize with its hatred of imperialism, we cannot support its repression of the Gospel.

There is a great tendency for liberal white westerners—including many Christians—to be so enamored of the liberation movements in developing nations that they neglect to consider whether that movement is moving people further away from God. A regime that harasses and imprisons Christians is equally guilty, whether it does so in the name of black nationalism or the name of Marxist communism. The sad truth is that many liberation movements have sold their souls to the Revolution. In their understandable rage and frustration after years of anti-black suffering, they have too often unleashed their own horrors on the people whom they set out to save. Their legacy to the African continent too often has been to continue the tradition of violence and tragic savagery in a new and more brutal way.

Perhaps the earliest of these bloody local wars came in the Congo (before it was known by its present name of Zaire), as Belgian authorities withdrew, and Patrice Lumumba began to seize power. A United Nations document provided this look at Lumumba's confidential instructions to heads of Congo's provinces:

> Terrorism is essential to subdue the population. Arrest all members of the opposition. Imprison the ministers, deputies, and senators. Do not spare them; revive the system of flogging. Inflict humiliation on the people thus arrested. For example, strip them in public, if possible in the presence of their wives and children. Those who do not succumb in prison should not be released for at least a year.

(The Western world responded to the bloodshed in the Congo by showing a cruel side of its own. The United Nations set up a detention camp in Katanga, and imprisoned thousands of Baluba tribesmen, most of whose only crime was to be members of the "wrong" tribe. Forty thousand civilians were jammed into a single camp. It became a ghetto, where no drainage system existed, and fifteen hundred tons of fecal matter accumulated. One thousand inmates died in the first three months.)

There is no monopoly on cruelty in Africa. No race, no political group can lift up hands which are clean of violence. It is a continent whose turbulent history seems to have elicited from whites and blacks, colonialists and revolutionaries, foreigners and natives the ugliest human qualities. It is impossible in modern Africa to take sides on the basis of absolute virtue. None seems to exist. Rather, the Christian responsibility is to demand of every government and movement that it provide its people a free opportunity to seek God and do the work of His Kingdom.

A Minority Takeover

When I see the constant, unrelenting march of communism into Africa, I think of a time when I spoke at a university in Alberta, Canada. I had been on tour of American colleges, in meetings set up by local Christian college fellowships. After I spoke, I opened the floor for questions, as I usually do, and immediately two young men stood and came from the back of the hall to the two microphones which had been placed on the main floor. Both were long-haired, bearded fellows who were dressed in a way that in those days marked them as radicals. In my spirit I said a quick prayer, because I sensed that they were going to give trouble. They immediately launched into a long attack on Christianity, a bitter diatribe that condemned Christians as racists and imperialists, while they sang the virtues of Marxism and Maoism. One would talk awhile, then the other.

I interrupted them and told them they had taken their share of the time, and should give opportunity for other students to ask questions. There were hundreds of Christian young people there, but my challenge was met with a deathly silence. The Christian kids were scared! I practically pleaded with them to come to the microphone and ask questions that would take the attention away from the radicals. But no one moved. The two Communist students started in again, and there was nothing I could do to stop them. They were about to take over the whole assembly.

Then, just when the situation seemed impossible, two students, one black and one white, got up and walked to the microphones. Each joined one of the Marxists at each microphone. The black student spoke first: "I am from

Nigeria," he started. "I would like to take this opportunity to thank the Christians who came to Africa to tell us about Jesus Christ. If they had not come, I would not be at this university. I would still be a savage and a heathen. I would be lost forever, and I am so grateful that missionaries came to turn us away from this godless Revolution." The radical beside him looked silently down at his feet.

Then immediately the white student began to speak. He was a refugee from Eastern Europe. "Because of the unbearable pressure from Communists, I was forced to flee my country," he said. "I am now free in this Christian country to do all the things I could not do in the land of my birth." It was perfect. He went on to tell of communism, and its repression of the people. He ended by saying, "I am glad I am in a free society where everyone can speak, including the Marxist, because in my Marxist homeland anyone who spoke out against Marxism was shot." When he finished, the crowd broke into thunderous applause, and the radical students turned without a word and almost ran out of the auditorium!

What a perfect example that was of a tiny Communist minority aggressively taking over a situation from hundreds of Christians—all because, for a while, no one would challenge them. Two Marxists intimidated four hundred Christians and almost succeeded in coming into *their* meeting and controlling it! They almost succeeded—not because of their superior strength—but because of the weakness of the Christians, the silent majority. They moved. They acted. They seized the opening and almost got away with it. It took two outsiders, one from Europe and one from Africa, to turn things around.

If the Communists win Africa, it will be by that same

pattern, by being aggressive when we are passive, by pressing their claims while we are silent with ours, by moving into the vacuum while we are afraid to step forward.

I refute the statement that communism is the church's number one enemy. There is a much bigger enemy than that. The church can survive under any political regime—but it cannot survive under apathy. That is the greatest enemy.

The battle can only be won by those who are willing to fight!

7

How to Destroy a Church

The reason we must oppose the spread of the Revolution in Africa is simply because the Revolution seeks to destroy the church.

That may seem very simple to you, but amazingly many Christians do not believe it. Especially outside the traditional Christian countries of Europe and North America, many people object to the fight of the church against communism. "Isn't it true that the Christian message is nonpolitical," they say, "and therefore it is compatible with any political system?" "Can't a Christian be a good Socialist or Communist," they argue. "Why do you get so overwrought about the Communists coming into Africa? Why not just preach the Gospel and let the political situation alone?"

Let me make it clear that I do not oppose communism as a political system, or as an economic system. I oppose it as a worldwide conspiracy against the church. Communism as an economic theory does not frighten me. It is communism as a religion that is dangerous, and communism is exactly that—a religion bent on owning men's minds and hearts. Wherever it spreads, it takes the place of other ideologies and religious beliefs. It has its own counterfeit for almost every Christian doctrine and practice. It has several Messiahs—Marx, Lenin, and Mao. It has a doctrine of conversion—the repentance for sins "against the people" and commitment to the cause of Revolution. It has a body of "scripture"—Mao's *Red Book* and the writings of Marx and Lenin. It has a tradition of evangelism—the drive for worldwide Revolution that has Russian, Chinese, and Cuban young people all around the globe working for it.

Revolutionary communism is not only a religion, it is an extremely intolerant religion. It fights every other religion with unrelenting malice, and that makes the Christian church its constant enemy. It seeks to squeeze the life out of the church, because it has correctly identified Christian faith as the only force on earth capable of beating it.

I am appalled at the trend in America and Western Europe to dismiss the Revolution as a tame, toothless adversary. The politics of détente has lulled us to sleep. It is no longer fashionable to oppose the communistic menace. Even in our churches we are assured that "things are better" behind the Iron Curtain, that Christians are not suffering so much anymore, that all the talk of smuggling Bibles and praying for imprisoned Christians is just so much romantic nonsense. I recently heard a tape recording of a speech made in a Baptist church in Texas. Three Russian pastors were there, describing the condition of the church behind the Iron Curtain, and they solemnly assured the audience that there was no persecution of Christians in Russia, that everyone has freedom to worship as he chooses, that there was no need to smuggle Bibles into the country.

When I heard that tape, I felt great sadness for those three pastors, because I know the pressure they are under. I know that what they were saying was the lie of the state, and they were pitifully betraying the truth, for whatever reasons. I do not condemn those men. They are victims, as far as I am concerned, and not villains. They live day to day in the presence of the Soviet police, while I sit comfortably in the freedom of Holland, so who am I to judge them or condemn them?

But their message, whatever its source, is not true! I have been there, many times over, for a dozen years in dozens of towns and villages, and I know that the church in Communist lands is suffering great persecution—now, today, while you read these words. The Revolution is the enemy of the church. It has always been and will always be. The confusion on this point that seems to prevail in the West—especially in America—is a tragic development that will contribute to even greater suffering of our brothers and sisters in controlled countries.

Alexander Solzhenitsyn is certainly no wide-eyed evangelical sensationalist. He must surely be accepted as a credible person in describing the state of affairs in his country: "The authorities continue to oppress and persecute the Russian church with the same arrogant, atheistic malice," he says in *Solzhenitsyn's Religion.* "They tolerate the church only to the extent that it is necessary for political decoration . . . ." That explains the occasional reassuring reports that come from Russia, telling us that all is well. Mark it down: Whenever we are told of particular churches or ministers who are faring well under the Revolution, it is an example of the "political decoration" of which Solzhenitsyn speaks. The suffering of the vast majority of Christians is as severe as it ever was.

The prayers of fellow Christians are the lifeline of the suffering church, and Satan knows that if free-world Christians can be convinced there is no problem, convinced that a sense of urgency is an outmoded "cold war" attitude, then the suffering church loses its main source of support. And so a campaign to hide the truth continues. For example, there was much ado made recently over the announcement that fifty thousand Bibles were being printed by the Romanian government. That was all window dressing. What the public was not told is that the Bibles were printed in a language that the common people cannot read, in a version which is totally unacceptable to Protestants, and every person getting a copy must register with the police!

Such examples abound. The Russians announced a few years ago that sixty Baptists were being released from prison before their sentences were completed. They announced this as if it were worthy of great applause, as if it showed them to be great humanitarians. Yet before that announcement, they had insisted that no Baptists were in jail at all! And no one is able to ask the important question: If you let sixty go, how many are still behind bars? Another time I heard a Soviet official boast: "Of course we have plenty of Bibles in Russia! Only last year we allowed the Bible Society to send in over three thousand copies." And I thought, "Three thousand copies—in a country of a quarter of a billion people!" Still they can claim that their government does not forbid the importing of Bibles.

The idea that communism no longer engages in repression of the church is a dangerously inaccurate one. Wherever there is a revolutionary government, there are several basic kinds of repression.

YOUTH. The government forbids young people from joining the church until they are eighteen, and forbids catechism classes and Christian education programs. In China, students attending the state universities were forbidden even to give thanks to God for their food, and were eventually disqualified from receiving scholarship grants unless they renounced their faith.

LITERATURE. Christian literature is against the law in many places. In others it is not illegal to own it, but to publish or import it. In Poland, for example, the church is allowed to publish only one religious book per year. In many countries there are a few Bibles scattered prominently around the major tourist cities, but nothing at all in the small towns, where most of the people live and are much easier to control. In Russia, every printing machine is state-owned, and a group of Christians who were caught operating a small press recently are still in prison for it.

WORSHIP. Churches are allowed to remain open in most places, but are severely restricted in their operation. In Romania it is illegal to have more than one service per week. In Vietnam since the Communist takeover, churches are limited to one meeting for one hour each week. And even then services are often disturbed or broken up by the police, particularly if there is a significant revival spirit that is making an impact on that particular area. As long as a church consists only of a couple of elderly people meeting quietly together, not reaching out for new people, the state is more likely to leave them alone, then proclaim to the world that it allows total freedom of worship.

Persecution in Africa

There is enormous evidence that in Africa the Revolution is following the predictable pattern. As the Revolution overwhelms a country, the church is caught in the grip of repression and persecution.

In *Uganda,* the regime of Idi Amin engages in wholesale murder and persecution of Christians. Most Christian schools have been closed or taken over by the government. The church continues to operate, but is crippled by lack of vehicles or equipment to get Bibles to the bush country where most of the people live. One Bible Society leader in Kampala joked to me, "I read in my Bible that God owns the cattle on a thousand hills [Psalms 50:10]. I wish He could sell some of His cattle and give us auto parts!"

The church in *Angola* has been recently closed entirely, and now seems to be opening up again. The Cuban-led MPLA engages in a familiar revolutionary pattern—alternately harassing the church and ignoring it, creating fear and tension.

In *Tanzania,* our ministry alone has sent fifty thousand New Testaments, printed in the Chinese language, into the labor camps where Chinese laborers lived while building the Tan-Zam Railway. How did we get them in? We printed the Scriptures inside a small red-backed handbook made to look exactly like the famous *Red Book* of Chairman Mao.

Christians in *Rwanda* are severely restricted. The president of the country is a Catholic, but still students, even in the capital city, are not allowed to go to church on Sunday.

In *Mozambique,* the overthrow of the government by the revolutionary FRELIMO has brought severe persecution. An estimated one hundred fifty missionaries were thrown into prison; all mission schools were nationalized; Christian holidays have been struck off the calendar. An official government statement declared: "The people must learn to understand that going to church or obeying the preaching of missionaries involves working against Mozambique and serving imperialist powers."

I recently heard by tape from a black Mozambican Christian who had been thrown into prison for handing out gospel tracts on the street. He was in prison for a year and a half, and has just been released. He managed to slip a small portion of the Scriptures into jail with him, and testified that through that Scripture—the Book of Jeremiah—God made the time in jail one of great spiritual growth. The man had a ONE-WAY Christian sweatshirt on when he was arrested, and his fellow prisoner gave him the nickname "One-Way." In the year and a half he led many of them to Christ.

In the *Sudan,* the only religious publishing house in the country was put out of operation by the government. Permits must be obtained for all church meetings, and lists submitted of those planning to attend. Catechism classes are forbidden in many districts, except by special permission.

In *Equatorial Guinea,* under an almost totally Marxist regime, it has been reported that five thousand people have been murdered since 1971, mostly on the grounds of their Catholic faith. Most churches are now used as warehouses, religious education has been stopped, and priests have been forbidden to express any criticism of the government.

To anticipate what will happen if the Revolution overruns the continent, we can look to what has happened in Southeast Asia. John Kearn watched the subtle and skillful crippling of the church there, and describes a sad, familiar progression of events. The revolutionaries at first agree for church services to continue, but insist that in return the Christians must not talk about religion outside the church. Witnessing dries up. House meetings become impossible. "We are being reasonable," they say. "We allow your worship in church, but you must not gather in homes, as part of the bargain." Then they cut down on the permissible meeting times, then begin taking the names of people who attend, and those people begin losing their jobs and suffering harassment from the government.

After a few months they say, "We have nationalized the banks and the industries. We want to nationalize the church, too, to show that we are cooperating with it." So the church is dedicated to the state—"in name only," they are assured—and a government official is named "president" of the church in order to supervise it. (It does, after all, now belong to the state.) Soon he announces that all pastors must register with the government, and that Christian literature will be restricted because it is a holdover from the old days of colonial imperialism. And a bit later the kids start coming from school singing familiar tunes of the church, with new revolutionary lyrics. Eventually some courageous Christian raises his voice against all this and denounces the state for attacking the church, and he is arrested and sent to a labor camp for two years. The charge: working to subvert the government. And finally the so-called president of the church announces that the mission in your village is being closed, so that the building may be used by the state. "Don't be alarmed," he assures the villagers. "There is a church still open where you can worship, only seventy miles away in the big city, one day a week." And by then there is not a voice raised against it.

Can it happen? That entire sequence of events—and more—occurred in a span of *just one year* in Laos in 1976.

Make no mistake about it. The Revolution still destroys the church, wherever it has the power to do so.

8

The Bloodiest of Them All

In the battle for Africa, there are many battlegrounds, and the bloodiest of them all in the late 1970s is the small, land-locked country of Uganda.

In Uganda, the suffering church is a reality—a fact of life. On any given day, when Christians in America and Europe are sitting down to thank the Lord for their bacon and eggs, it is likely that somewhere in Uganda a fellow believer is being beaten or jailed or killed because of his Christian identity.

The terror which now rules Uganda demonstrates again the mind-boggling speed with which conditions can change in Africa. Books written a few years ago about the African crisis did not even mention Uganda as a potential trouble area. It seemed a progressive, relatively peaceful nation, where communism has little appeal and the Christian church is well established. Uganda seemed a cool spot in a hot African map. But, with dizzying speed, all that has changed. An unexpected military coup. Takeover by a fierce, anti-Christian minority. A half-mad dictator named Idi Amin. And suddenly the church and hundreds of thousands of Christians are plunged into an atmosphere of persecution and fear.

Uganda is a land of spectacular beauty, just mountainous enough to give variety and color to its lush tropical countryside. It lies by the side of Lake Victoria, the largest body of fresh water on the continent, where a single brilliant Ugandan sunset is said to be worth a trip there to see. Kampala, a city which, like Rome, sits on seven hills, has for many years been one of Africa's leading capitals, a modern and prosperous focal point of local energies and Western investment. The city boasts of Makerere University, for many years the leading (at one time the only) university in East Africa. The gorgeous game reserves in the bush country north of Kampala have always been regarded as among the most beautiful in Africa, and for many decades have attracted tourists from around the world.

The natural beauties of Uganda are still there, to be sure, but much of the old Uganda has been swept away by the country's current upheaval. In downtown Kampala, the once-bustling life of the city has come to a virtual standstill. Stores stand open with few consumer goods on the shelves. A public transport system that once numbered several hundred vehicles has dwindled until there are reportedly only about a dozen buses in operation in the entire country. (One soccer field in Kampala is filled with abandoned buses, unusable for lack of spare parts.) The nation's coffee crop, for many years its leading export, goes unharvested. A large, modern terminal building at Entebbe Airport is an empty shell, all but deserted with only an occasional trickle of passengers moving through large, unused spaces. The Ugandan shilling is becoming increasingly worthless, and many goods can no longer be purchased except with black-market foreign currency.

A Ugandan was quoted in an American paper recently:

"I'm sorry you could not have seen Uganda a few years ago. This was such a pleasant place. Maybe Uganda will be born again. What you see now is not Uganda." And so the Europeans and other foreigners have fled the country in the past two years, often leaving their belongings behind, leaving in such numbers that there are now only a few hundred whites left in the entire country. The few East African Airways flights that leave Entebbe Airport each week always include westerners on a one-way ticket out.

What they are leaving behind is twelve million Ugandans who cannot flee. They stay on in a climate of growing fear and repression. I slipped into Kampala quietly a few months ago to meet with some Christian brethren. I was met by a Ugandan clergyman at the airport and cleared the passport control with a "visitor's pass" which limited my activity to three days' "sightseeing." We began to converse as he pulled our car away from the airport, when he suddenly cut me short: "We are being followed by the police. Just look straight ahead and talk naturally. Nothing to be alarmed about, but you should know." And, though he tried to relax and urged me to do the same, the tension and sense of foreboding were real and constant in that city.

Many conversations are whispered conversations in Uganda these days. "People just disappear," one Ugandan told me. "They just disappear, and nobody ever sees them again."

The architect of this tragic new Uganda is a man who likes to be addressed as *His Excellency Al-Haji Field Marshal Dr. Idi Amin Dada, V.C., D.S.O., M.C., Life President of Uganda.* To the rest of the world, he is *Big Daddy* Amin. To many Americans and Europeans, he is a cartoon character—a joke. It is easy to laugh at him from the detached comfort of the Western world. But to Christians in Uganda, there is nothing funny about Idi Amin.

Amin is a large, robust soldier who rules Uganda with an army of twenty thousand well-equipped men. He became president in 1971 by overthrowing the government of President Milton Obote, who now lives in exile in Tanzania. Amin pours millions of dollars into his army while the country staggers under a failing economy. A large secret police force helps him stay in power by jailing or killing those who object to his policies, operating in Gestapo-like fashion with what seems to be unlimited power. Estimates of the number of people killed by Amin's so-called "Security Forces" range between 100 thousand and 300 thousand, and reports filter out of the country of torture, mass executions, and the constant discoveries of bullet-riddled bodies floating in the crocodile-infested Nile River.

The major target in this nightmare of terror is the Christian church. Amin is a Muslim, and in recent years has looked to the Arab world for military and financial support for his troubled regime. Muslims comprise only about 6 percent of the Uganda population—another example of the power of an aggressive minority—compared to a Christian majority that can be conservatively estimated at 60 percent. But it is Amin and the Muslims who have the guns, and Christians seem unable to protect themselves against the brutal Muslim dictator.

Like so much of the violence in Africa, the Ugandan persecutions spring partly from tribal rivalry. Amin's small Kakwa tribe, known for its fierce, warring history, is a traditional enemy of the Acholi and Langi tribes, which include most of the country's better educated business and professional leaders. The Acholis and Langis are also predominantly Christian; the Kakwas, largely Muslim. It is easy for Western outsiders to underestimate the importance of African tribal differences in current political events; but, to some modern-day Africans, tribal loyalty still is a powerful influence, and in this case it combines with Amin's anti-Christian bias to produce a dangerous climate for hundreds of thousands of Ugandan Christians. Until last year, Ugandan church leaders were reluctant to label the repressive conditions in their country as *persecution*, perhaps fearing reprisal and even greater difficulty if such statements reached Amin's ears. Amin has always been sensitive to his negative image in the world community, and has reacted violently to criticism of his regime. But in 1976 and '77 the situation for Christians became worse, and now Ugandan church leaders are fleeing the country in large numbers and are spreading the word that in Uganda today it can be dangerous—even fatal—to be an outspoken Christian disciple. But there are still such disciples in Uganda, outspoken Christians, willing to risk everything for the Kingdom.

A dramatic example is that of Janani Luwum, who was Archbishop of the (Anglican) church of Uganda and the country's highest-ranking Protestant leader. Luwum was a popular fifty-three-year-old archbishop. I visited him in Kampala in November of 1976, and discussed with him the need for more Bibles for Ugandans. He was training chaplains for the Ugandan Army at that time, and the spiritual needs of Amin's soldiers were heavy on his heart. We made plans to ship ten thousand copies of new Bibles to him for distribution to the soldiers. He was a man of great warmth, a man who exuded a sense of love and compassion. Though he was officially titled "His Grace, The Most Reverend Janani Luwum, Archbishop of Uganda, Rwanda, Burundi, and Boga-Zaire," with the two of us it was simply "Brother!" We were remarkably one in the Spirit.

Luwum became a minister during the East African revival which swept Uganda before Amin came to power, and rose rapidly through the ranks of the church, becoming the archbishop in 1974 at a ceremony in Kampala's Namirembe Cathedral. A photograph of the ceremony still hangs in the conference room of the Church of Uganda, showing Luwum in the flowing purple robes of his office, with a smiling Idi Amin offering congratulations.

But that was in earlier and better days. As the pattern of violence against Christians developed in the years since then, relationships between Amin and the country's spiritual leader became increasingly strained. The plight of Luwum and other church leaders was a familiar one in countries where the church is suffering: to speak out against the persecution was to incur greater hostility, and even personal danger to Luwum himself. As more Christians disappeared in 1976, Luwum began to risk increasingly open criticism of the Amin regime. In his traditional Christmas message, which was broadcast throughout the nation, he expounded the theme that the only victory for Christians was sometimes that of "suffering in love." That statement was regarded as a political comment by the government officials who monitored the broadcast, and Luwum was abruptly cut off the air in mid-sermon.

On a Saturday night in early February, a squad of Amin's secret police broke down the fence surrounding Luwum's residence, forced their way into his house with loaded rifles, and accused Luwum of hiding weapons. He tells the story himself:

> At about 1:30 A.M. I heard the dog barking wildly and the fence being broken down and I knew someone had come into the compound . . . When I opened the door, immediately these armed men who had been hiding sprang on me, cocking their rifles and shouting, "Archbishop, Archbishop, show us the arms." At this point their leader, who was speaking in Arabic, wearing a red kaunda suit, put his rifle in my stomach while another searched me from head to foot. He pushed me with the rifle shouting "Walk, run, show us the arms, take us to your bedroom!" So we went up to our bedroom where Mary, my wife, was asleep. They woke her up and began crawling underneath the bed.

The intruders searched the entire house, virtually tearing it apart, but found nothing. They searched the chapel, looked under the Holy Communion table, broke into sacks of millet and groundnuts in the storage rooms, even searched in the toilets in each bathroom. Frustrated at finding nothing, they asked Luwum: "Tell us the location of any Acholi or Langi homes in Namirembe (the hill on which the Cathedral stands) so that they may be searched."

Luwum answered them: "I did not come to Namirembe for the Acholi or for the Langi. I am the Archbishop of Uganda, Rwanda, Burundi, and Boga-Zaire. Our house is God's house, and there are no arms in God's house! We pray for the President. We pray for the Security Forces—whatever they do. We preach the Gospel and we pray for others. That is our work, not keeping arms!"

At 3:00 A.M. the search finally ended and the men left. Luwum recounted their departure: "They asked us to open the gate for them to go out, but my wife suggested they should go out the way they came. I said we were Christians. We have clean hearts, and as a witness to them we would open the gates for them. We did and they drove away."

On the same night another Anglican bishop, Yona Okoth of Bukedi, was similarly awakened and his house searched. He was ordered to leave his house with the men, as he described it: "Their leader said, 'We have been given a directive from our boss. We are sorry but we shall have to take you.' I replied, 'I'm not afraid. If it is death for me it is the gateway to the Lord. If life, I will continue preaching the Gospel.' " Okoth was interrogated throughout the night, then returned to his home and released the next morning. A third Christian was taken from his home and has not been seen or heard from since that night.

Four days later, eighteen Uganda bishops met to draft a letter of protest to Amin. Citing the Saturday-night incidents as examples, the letter went on to object to Amin's reign of terror, perhaps the sharpest protest ever made up to that time by Christians still living in the country:

> The gun whose muzzle has been pressed against the Archbishop's stomach, the gun which has been used to search the Bishop of Bukedi's house is a gun which is being pointed at every Christian in the church. The security of the ordinary Christian has been in jeopardy for quite a long time. It may be that what has happened to the archbishop and the bishop of Bukedi is what is consistently happening to our Christians. *We have buried many* who have died as a result of being shot, and there are many more whose bodies have not been found, yet

> their disappearance is connected with the activities of some members of the Security Forces. Your Excellency, if it is required we can give concrete evidence of what is happening, because widows and orphans are members of our Church . . . In some parts of Uganda members of Islam who are in leading positions are coercing Christians into becoming Muslims . . . While you, Your Excellency, have stated that your government is not under any foreign influence, the general trend of things in Uganda has created a feeling that the affairs of our nation are being directed by outsiders who do not have the welfare of this country and the value of the lives of Ugandans at their heart.

I have read the entire text of the five-page letter, and I marvel at such a courageous statement by a group of ministers, each of whom, as he signed the letter, must have known that he was incurring the anger of a dangerous dictator with power of life and death over each of his twelve million subjects. Luwum personally delivered the letter to President Amin, and sent copies to political and religious leaders throughout Uganda.

Amin's reaction to the bold protest was swift and violent. Two days later he held a frenzied military rally in Kampala, ordering Luwum to appear to be charged with attempting to overthrow the government. Over one hundred Chinese automatic weapons, thousands of rounds of ammunition, and hundreds of hand grenades were displayed as evidence of "smuggled weapons" which Luwum and his friends were accused of hiding. For over four hours the soldiers—all handpicked Amin loyalists—listened to speeches condemning the church leaders. They chanted and roared, "Kill them! Kill them!" when asked what should be done with those who plot against Amin.

After the rally, Luwum and two government ministers were arrested and taken away from the site in an army vehicle. The next day, Radio Uganda announced that they had been killed in an auto accident. Luwum's body was never returned to Kampala. Eyewitnesses reported seeing the body with three bullet holes, two in the chest and one in the mouth. One Anglican minister who recently fled the country told me personally that the car which was allegedly involved in the crash had actually been wrecked earlier, and had been in a garage awaiting repairs for several weeks before the Luwum death.

As other refugees fled the country, more details emerged. *Christianity Today* (March 18, 1977) summed them up in this report:

> Amin ordered all three shot, they said, and the two government officials were promptly killed. When the president learned that his troops were reluctant to shoot the archbishop he is reported to have shot Luwum himself. Soldiers were also reported to have been reluctant to follow Amin's order to run trucks over the bodies of the three; they finally agreed to crush the corpses of the cabinet members but not the archbishop's.
>
> Family members and church officials asked for the archbishop's body after the deaths were announced, but they were not permitted . . . . Instead the government sent the coffin to Luwum's

> native village in northern Uganda. Relatives and friends were instructed to bury him, but they delayed until they could call in a priest to conduct a funeral. At that time the coffin was opened, and bullet wounds were found.

Around the world, no one was buying Amin's car-crash story. In Geneva, Switzerland, The International Commission of Jurists declared the deaths an assassination, stating that "the pretense that they were killed in a motor accident will deceive no one." A group of Ugandan exiles in the United States called the murders "part of a calculated plan to exterminate Christianity" in their country. Andrew Young, the U.S. Ambassador to the United Nations, flatly declared that the evidence showed the death of Luwum to be an assassination. And in every part of the globe, rage and disbelief at the murders filled the newspapers and airwaves. President Jimmy Carter declared that Amin's murders had "disgusted the entire civilized world."

Final confirmation of the murders came in June of 1977, when Henry Kyemba, the Ugandan Minister of Health and a friend of Amin for twenty years, fled the country and told the whole story. He listed dozens of other leading Ugandan citizens whose murders he personally knew of, and said, "It is a very agonizing situation: no one can speak of it in Uganda and expect to remain alive."

The Luwum death triggered a bloody wave of new killings in Uganda. Amin ordered a fresh sweep of Christians from positions of importance, especially in the army, and an estimated three thousand victims were killed within a month of Luwum's death. Hundreds of Ugandans escaped the country, many of them traveling through the forests and bush to unmarked border crossings into Kenya and Rwanda.

One such refugee was a young Ugandan with whom I had shared fellowship only three months earlier in his home in Kampala. I saw him in Holland after his escape and heard him speak of the horrors which he had left behind. I thought of the comfortable home he had abandoned, forced to flee overland to escape the Security Forces. I remembered the prayers we prayed together, and how fervently he was working for the spread of the Kingdom in his homeland. How little he knew then that within half a year he would meet me again in Europe, this time not as a church official but as a refugee, as a man—at least temporarily—without a country.

But that is the way of Africa. That is the volatile, violent nature of a continent which has become a spiritual battlefield between the forces of Darkness and Light. Today a Kampala suburbanite—tomorrow a refugee. Today a democracy—tomorrow a police state. Today a wife—tomorrow a widow. Today an archbishop—tomorrow a martyr.

In such a chaotic land, only the power of the Spirit and the presence of Christ is certain. In a land where death is a constant companion, can there be true Christian love? Is the message of Christ really relevant there? Is it really reasonable to expect a man to love his enemies, to pray for those who abuse and persecute him, to embrace those who come calling in the dead of night with guns and knives? Festo Kivengere thinks so. He was one of the bishops who signed Luwum's protest letter, and afterwards eluded the Security Forces in a frightening midnight escape through the countryside. Safely out of the country of his birth, Festo wrote these words for *Christianity Today* (April 15, 1977):

> I love Idi Amin. I have never been his enemy. I wish somebody would take the message back to him. If I were in Uganda, I would shout it from the housetops. If I could get near President Amin, I would tell him to his face . . . . Forgiveness is creative. Retaliation is destructive. Anyone who loves humanity must seek the constructive, reconciling way. God did it. Who am I to stray from His way? So that is why I love Idi Amin. Love can heal, and I will be committed to that until I die.

9

One Nation *Could* Save All of Africa

"It is a paradise on earth."

"The place is a prison camp. It is a festering sore on the face of humanity."

What you have just read are two descriptions of the same place: the southern African country of Rhodesia. Such differing viewpoints, each as emotional as the other, only hint at the divisive, explosive presence of Rhodesia and neighboring South Africa on the contemporary African landscape. South Africa and Rhodesia are not merely countries anymore; they have become symbols to people on both sides of the African struggle. To their white citizens, and many other whites besides, they have become symbols of a determined, never-say-die refusal to surrender to blacks their hard-won stake in the African continent. To most blacks in Africa, and many other people around the world, they have become symbols of the arrogant, unlawful domination of black Africans on their own soil.

How to solve that highly charged impasse has become a thorny and critical dilemma in the battle for Africa.

In both countries, a small white minority governs, with little participation by black African citizens. In both cases, this white minority grants to itself privileges and opportunities which it does not extend to blacks, and keeps black and white sharply separated both by law and by a deeply entrenched social tradition. In each case the white government has withstood a growing storm of criticism and repudiation by most of the rest of the world, making changes in the established order only very reluctantly, despite a rising tide of unrest from its own black population.

But, along with these obvious similarities, there are several critical differences between the two countries, and it is becoming increasingly difficult to discuss the two situations as a single problem.

Rhodesia

A friend of mine, who has traveled in many troubled areas around the globe, told me early this year, "I have never seen any place in the world so ideally suited for terrorism as Rhodesia. It couldn't be better suited for guerrilla warfare, if it were *made* for that purpose."

And Rhodesia has plenty of guerrilla warfare. In the past few years its black population—they outnumber the ruling whites by 23 to 1—has turned increasingly to violence to force the government to surrender its control of the country. President Ian Smith leads the government, which in 1965 renounced its status as a British colony and declared itself an independent republic, rather than bow to British demands for Rhodesian blacks to be given a wider role in national leadership. Most of the nations of the world have boycotted Rhodesia since that time, challenging its legality, and refusing, at least officially, to buy its products. In the meantime, the rising tide of black nationalism has gradually encircled the country. It shares long borders with hostile Zambia, Botswana, and Mozambique, which openly give support, shelter, and arms to the roving bands of terrorists who vow to chase the white "intruders" from their land.

Inside Rhodesia, a fortress mentality has developed. The whites feel cut off from the rest of the world, with little to sustain them but their own grim determination to survive. They travel from town to town in motor convoys to protect themselves from guerrilla attack. Farmhouses are ringed by high fences and alarm systems, with radio communications connecting each house to the nearest police station. From the capital city of Salisbury, officials ponder ways to stanch the flow of whites from the country. They are departing now at the rate of eleven hundred per month, and heavy military call-ups and higher taxes seem sure to make the exodus even worse.

There will be more bloodshed in Rhodesia before the issue is finally settled, and almost everyone agrees that all-out war between the white government and black nationalist forces could erupt at any time. One factor that slows progress toward a compromise settlement is the division among the blacks themselves. There are four major factions, ranging from the relatively moderate followers of Bishop Abel Muzorewa to the militant Patriotic Front, led by Joshua Nkomo and Robert Mugabe. It is a reasonable fear of Rhodesian whites that, even if black majority rule is accomplished peacefully, the factionalism of the blacks will trigger a bloody battle for control.

As is always the case, the Revolution has seized upon the Rhodesian conflict and used it to create turmoil and division. The constant strain of terrorism and fear has set one part of the church against another, isolating Christians and paralyzing the effective spread of the Kingdom. The divisions are deep and bitter. The white Catholic bishop of Umtali, the Reverend Donal Lamont, was sentenced last year to ten years in prison for neglecting to report the presence of revolutionaries in his area. He represents a growing—though still small—number of Rhodesian clergymen who believe the government policy to be wrong and unchristian; and his treatment by the authorities served to sharpen the agony of a divided church.

In Rhodesia, many individual Christians have experienced miracles delivering them from injury and death at the hands of guerrillas. There have been cases of grenades failing to explode, of guerrillas being miraculously diverted when death seemed a certainty, and other extraordinary experiences. Several Rhodesians have told me such stories, interpreting these events to mean that God is on the side of the whites and will not let the white regime fall. This is a sad mistake, I fear, and one that was often made in Southeast Asia. During the war in Vietnam, I worked with a village of tribesmen which was once totally surrounded by protecting angels, visible to the Viet Cong, and was saved from destruction. I believe that such things do truly occur, and I praise the Lord for His protection of Christian people in such cases in Rhodesia. But Vietnam fell to the Revolution like an overripe fruit when the time came, and those who accepted the miracles there as a sign that South Vietnam would prevail were greatly disillusioned. I believe that such miracles are meant for individual Christians, perhaps even for the purpose of inspiring and encouraging them for a time ahead more difficult than anyone but God can know. To interpret them as a sign that the country will not fall to the Revolution is a sad mistake.

I have been in Rhodesia, have met with the prime minister, and talked with many wonderful Christians. The reliance on the hand of God that one might wish to find in such a difficult area seems, except in some individual cases, to be missing in the attitude of the white population as a whole. There is instead a mingling of stubborn intransigence (I suppose it might more generously be called *determination*) and a kind of fatalism that whatever will be, will be.

Black Rhodesians, factionalized as they are, are in agreement on the new name for Rhodesia once they have gained control. *Zimbabwe* they will call it. (The name is derived from two Shona words that mean *venerated houses*, referring to a cluster of enormous stone ruins presumably left by an advanced African culture hundreds of years ago.) The world may as well get accustomed to the sound of *Zimbabwe*, for unless there is a dramatic and unforeseen reversal of Rhodesia's fortunes, that is what we all shall be calling it before many days have passed.

South Africa

Further south, bordering Rhodesia, in the nation of South Africa, the outlook is not nearly so predictable. Both from a human standpoint and from a spiritual one, the prospects of escaping bloodshed and upheaval seem brighter.

Speaking in sheer human terms, the government in South Africa has several advantages over its Rhodesian counterpart: (1) The numerical imbalance is somewhat less extreme, with over four million whites in a total population of twenty-two million. (2) South Africa is much more highly developed technologically, with ten cities of 100 thousand plus population and correspondingly greater industrialization. (3) It has access to the sea—plenty of it, in fact, since it occupies the entire southern tip of the continent. (4) Its nonwhite population participates more fully in the life of the country, and generally has received more educational, medical, and occupational advantages than have the blacks of Rhodesia.

Still, these are "advantages" only in the very narrow sense that South Africa's situation is less precarious than Rhodesia's. In combination, they might add up to long-range survival for the South African nation, and they might serve only to delay its demise. That is impossible to say.

The greatest hope that South Africa can avoid bloodshed and upheaval does not rest with these flimsy human assets, however, but with a spiritual one. I believe that God has a special interest in the survival of the South African nation. There it is—controversial view, no doubt—but one which I believe deeply, and which I feel to be critical to one's overall view of the church in Africa. I believe that there is a special place in God's plan for South Africa, not necessarily a white-dominated South Africa, nor a black-dominated South Africa, but a strong, healthy South African nation where both blacks and whites live and work side by side to evangelize the rest of the continent.

I believe in a concept which might be called *regional evangelism*. God has given certain countries the primary responsibility for the evangelizing of the region of the world which they occupy. This regional responsibility is not something that is fixed from the beginning of time, something that has been a part of some predestined plan. It is rather a responsibility that emerges as history progresses. To whom much is given, much is expected, it is said. And certain countries find themselves at this point in history responsible for broad geographic areas, by virtue of greater strength and their potential ability to reach those areas for God. The Great Commission charges every Christian to go into "all the world," and a specific regional burden does not replace that global responsibility, but is added to it.

In today's world, I believe that the evangelization of Eastern Europe is the special responsibility of Western Europe. The United States is responsible for Central and South America. The burden for reaching all of Asia falls to Australia and New Zealand. And the continent of Africa is the special spiritual responsibility of South Africa.

Why? Because South Africa has the tools to reach the entire continent. It has the money, technology, large number of committed Christians, the freedom and political stability. It has everything needed to evangelize the continent of Africa, to equip black Africans in other countries to participate in that process, and to get the job done all the way from the Sahara Desert to the Cape of Good Hope. And I further believe that God will intervene in the course of history to preserve South Africa, if her people will accept her responsibility to evangelize the rest of the continent.

But first, the South African people—black and white alike—must accept that responsibility and join hands to accomplish it. Historically, the South Africans have never taken that task as seriously as they must if God is to preserve their nation. For three hundred and fifty years, South African whites have been on the continent, certainly long enough to make them native to it. They are not transplants or intruders, any more than the Americans are foreign to their continent, or the Brazilians are intruders in their land. They are truly Africans in a sense that cannot be claimed by any other whites on the continent. But they have never abandoned their basic *us-against-them* posture toward black Africans to the north, and that has kept them from taking full responsibility for the evangelizing of Africa. Now they have been isolated by the black nationalism that has swept Africa, have turned inward, thinking only of national survival. They have lost the vision that black Africans are their brothers, and the partners with whom they share a continent. They have come to regard black Africa as their *problem,* and not as their *opportunity,* and therein lies the difficulty.

The South African church is responsible for the rest of Africa because it is the strongest segment of the church on the African continent. I have written earlier of my great admiration for South African Christians. When I have presented the needs of the suffering church there, the response has been greater than anywhere in the world I have been. Within two years of opening an office there, Open Doors had more subscribers to its prayer letter than it has in Holland after *twenty* years!

During the 1972 Olympics in Munich, one of the largest contingents of young people in the witnessing team there was from South Africa, both black and white. At the 1976 Montreal Olympics, this witnessing effort was repeated, and the South African group—which was sponsored by Open Doors, incidentally—was second in size only to that of the USA. Last year the South African Bible Society topped every other country in the world, including the USA, in Bible distribution. Arthur Glasser, a missions leader who is by no means oversympathetic to the South African cause, reported early this year that in Stellenbosch University, with a total of eight thousand Afrikaaner students, thirty-six hundred meet weekly in over 600 student-led Bible study groups. He also reported that a single youth outreach ministry had some sixty young people spontaneously offer themselves for a year's work without pay in response to a recent challenge.

The South African church is one of tremendous devotion to Christ. It has the spiritual muscle and the financial resources to reach black Africa—if it will make that its overriding concern and obsession.

I believe Satan is aware that South Africa has this potential, and consequently works hard to isolate South Africa from the rest of the world. It has been singled out for boycott, embarrassment, and criticism, particularly, I believe, because Satan wants to isolate South Africa to prevent it from fulfilling its divine commission. (Much of the unpopularity which the United States experiences in the world community has the same origin. It has the manpower and spiritual resources to fulfill the Great Commission. All it lacks is the willpower. But if it can be criticized and harassed by world opinion sufficiently to drive it into a defensive shell, unwilling to make that commitment, then all its evangelistic potential can be neutralized.)

There is one great bridge which South Africa must cross before it can effectively meet the conditions for world evangelism. It must accept the black man as a fellow human being, embrace him as a brother, give him his dignity as a man. South African whites will argue that they have given the black man better medical care, better education, better housing and jobs, and more opportunities than any black government in Africa has given its citizens. They can point out that they have given him more human rights than he is likely to get anywhere else on the continent. But that is not the issue. The basic issue is human dignity, and white South Africans must give their black brothers that before their nation will be whole.

I once met with a group of white South African Christians who wanted to help me get Bibles into Russia. After they had shared with me their eagerness to help, I said, "Wait a minute. The first question is, have you given a Bible to your own black servants?"

They seemed surprised. "Well," they replied, "we have not, but the Bible is not available in their language."

There could be only one answer to that. I suspected that the so-called translation problem was only an excuse—that Bibles were indeed available in those languages—a fact that has since been confirmed by the Bible Society. "I don't want Russian Bibles from you if you haven't given the Word to your own black servants," I told them. "Africa is your first responsibility. Settle that problem first, and when you are doing what you can do here, we will work together to reach Russia."

If the whites of South Africa can meet the conditions and commit themselves totally to spreading the Gospel to black Africa, I am convinced that God will protect and preserve their nation. When they must turn their attention away from their own problems long enough to extend a spiritual hand to black Africa, then they will find their survival taking care of itself.

When I was a young soldier in the Dutch army, lying wounded in an Indonesian hospital bed, a Franciscan nun taught me a lesson. "Do you know how natives in this country catch monkeys?" she asked. I said I didn't. "They take a coconut and make a hole in it, just big enough for a monkey's paw to slip through. And then they drop a pebble into the hole and wait in the bushes with a net. Sooner or later, a curious monkey will come along. He will pick up the coconut and rattle it. He'll peer inside; and, then, he will slip his paw into the hole and get hold of that pebble. But when he tries to bring it out, he finds that he cannot get his paw through the hole without letting go. And he will simply not let go. He thinks he is holding something really valuable, and he will never let go of what he thinks is a prize. And then the natives drop the net over him. It is the easiest thing in the world to catch a fellow who acts like that."

The nun asked me: "Are you holding onto something, Andrew, something that is keeping you from your freedom?"

The white people of South Africa, faced with the difficult demands of their own peculiar dilemma, may well decide that there are things they must let go of, if they are to keep their freedom in their homeland.

10

What Can *You* Do?

I have often heard the story of the little Dutch boy who put his finger in the dike. No one knows if the story is true, but it is a favorite one nevertheless. The boy saw a tiny hole in the wall that holds back the sea, and by putting his finger in the hole until help arrived, he saved the entire country from a disastrous flood. The point of that little story is that even a small boy, by doing the right thing at the right time, could hold back the power of that enormous, frightening ocean.

I would not bother to tell you about Africa—if I did not believe that you can do something about it.

The prospect of a worldwide Revolution sweeping over an entire continent seems such a gigantic, cosmic threat that it might seem preposterous that a single individual could do anything to affect it one way or another. But the truth is that *you can personally make a difference in Africa.* Like the little Dutch boy at the dike, we Christians, by doing the right thing at the right time, can literally hold back the powerful, crushing flood of Revolution.

The reason we have this ability is that the battle for Africa is a *spiritual* battle, and in a spiritual battle only spiritual weapons count. If we believe the Bible, we must believe that a pitifully small boy named David whipped a monstrously large man named Goliath because their battle was decided spiritually. David recognized his fight with Goliath to be a spiritual one, and openly declared it to be so.

"Who is this uncircumcised Philistine, that he should defy the armies of the living God?" David cried (1 Samuel 17:26).

He fought Goliath because Goliath was an enemy of God. And he fought not for his own glory or pleasure, but for a purely spiritual purpose, ". . . that all the earth may know that there is a God in Israel" (1 Samuel 17:46). David won because his battle was a spiritual one.

Another reason we can make a difference is because the battle for Africa is an *undecided* one. The fight is far from over. Perhaps this book has emphasized the work of the enemy in Africa, but be assured that there are millions of dedicated Christians there who have still not conceded Africa to the Revolution. They are outnumbered and hard-pressed, but they are still there—and the battle is still undecided—so there is still time to help.

"What can I do?" you ask. "How can I *personally* make a difference?" You can help the cause of God in that continent by being willing to care, willing to learn, willing to suffer, willing to give, and willing to go.

Willing to Care

Are you really willing to care deeply about Africa? That will be a start, but it may not be as easy as it sounds. It is easy to pray a quick prayer for Africa and proceed with one's affairs without a second thought. For most of us, however, it is *hard work* to maintain an active concern for faraway people, when we have no direct interest at stake. It is easy to care about those things which threaten us directly, or from which there is promise of some direct payoff. But are we willing to force our attention toward Africa? Are we willing to ask God to burden us heavily, to break our hearts, for Africa?

In the past two decades, direct American corporate investment in black Africa has tripled. But has our missions giving tripled? Has the volume of our prayers tripled? Has the amount of time we spend seeking the Lord for Africa tripled? Of course not. It seems that the hope of making a profit motivates non-Christians more than the hope of spreading the Gospel motivates us. They care more than we do! I believe if the average Christian layman were told that he could double his money in a month's time by buying stock in the Zambian Copper Mining Corporation, and he invested a few thousand dollars in that company, he would suddenly take a great interest in southern Africa. He would check the paper every day to see if the value of that stock rose or fell. If news of events in Zambia flashed across the TV screen, he would yell for quiet and listen intently to understand what was happening in that part of the world. In other words, he would suddenly have a keen, constant interest in Zambia, simply because he had a few thousand dollars at stake. That is the kind of interest every Christian should take in Africa, where there hangs in the balance not money, but *four hundred million people,* and *indeed the momentum of the entire worldwide Revolution.*

It is this growing momentum which makes the African outcome so critical. Not just a single continent is at stake, but the larger global struggle as well. Africa is the hinge in the worldwide Revolution. Eastern Europe and Asia first, then Africa. If the Revolution succeeds there, it will swing, rapidly and with mounting force, to Latin America, making full the process of physical encirclement of the entire world. We must see that Africa is the hinge on which all else turns, and the future of not just the African church, but the church in the West as well, is threatened there.

I once conducted a meeting in a Protestant church in the United States. I presented the need of the suffering church and showed slides of the plight of Christians in Eastern Europe. We had a moving service, and people cried as I told them of their brothers and sisters under persecution. Then when I finished, they thanked me for being there, and took an offering to buy new cushions for the pews in their church. I could hardly believe it! I left empty-handed, while they bought new pew cushions. The people in that church cared enough to cry; they cared enough to experience an emotional twinge. But then when they had dried their tears, it was all over. They went ahead with their own concerns, their own comfort, business as usual. They were not willing to care enough to do something about the need.

Willing to Learn

After we have committed ourselves to caring, we must be willing to learn more about Africa. We must know what is happening there, otherwise how can we pray effectively, or give properly, or do what needs to be done? Too many Christians operate out of an intellectual vacuum—plenty of emotion, but no information. God wants you to be willing to learn about Africa, and that includes being open to all different sides of the issues there.

Suppose someone came to you and said, "I have a friend

whose name is Robert. Will you please pray for him?" What would you do? Assuming you are a person of faith and love, you would find a place of prayer, and you would begin to pray for Robert. But you wouldn't get very far. You would have a tough time maintaining your interest or your enthusiam, and your prayer would likely be a very short one indeed.

Why? Not because you are unconcerned about Robert, but because you simply do not know anything about him. After you have called his name a few times, and made some general appeals in his behalf, where would you go from there? Many Christians try to intercede for Africa that way. They have this vague idea that there is a place called Africa and it is filled with black people who need their prayers. That's about it. The serious, meaningful intervention in prayer that Africa needs from you is possible only if you are willing to learn about Africa. Only then can you put names, faces, and specific needs before your eyes when you pray.

Another reason we must be willing to learn about Africa is to make sure that our support goes to the right people. There is a growing church movement in Africa that seems more committed to the Revolution than to the Gospel. At a 1974 meeting of the All-Africa Conference of Churches, for example, delegates called for a moratorium on foreign missionaries, and applauded speakers who urged violence as a legitimate means of opposing white governments. One official of the organization stated that the presence of missionaries in Africa "enslaves African Christians," and the General Secretary of the conference declared: "The root of the African problem is the cultural arrogance of that small minority of mankind located in the North Atlantic world . . . ."

An African evangelical leader in attendance, Byang Kato, described the meeting:

> Poems on political liberation took the place of Bible reading. Delegates clamored until the early hours of the morning for a more violent approach on the matter of liberation. The meeting hall was decorated with pictures of the oppressed and of crusades for liberation. But I do not recall seeing any reference to sin as the fundamental dilemma of the human race, nor any call for the urgent task of bringing the salvation of Jesus Christ to both the sinful oppressed and the oppressor.

It is this brand of Christianity to which many Christians unwittingly give their support and money. Since 1972, the World Council of Churches has reportedly placed 1.2 million dollars at the disposal of African liberation movements, and has urged that churches support, as a last resort, revolutions and resistance movements in their fight against racism. The London *Daily Telegraph* has warned the public of this trend in an editorial which said, in part, "Once it was missionaries who received our support . . . now it is obscure, many-lettered organizations in Zambia and Tanzania who plant explosives by night and are the enemies of all peace and prosperity."

We must learn, also, from those Africans who can personally teach us about their continent and its unique problems. We must earn the right to their confidence by being willing to listen and prove our love with consistent concern and action. When Job's friends went to see him in his distress, they sat down for seven days without saying anything at all.

But after seven days they began to talk, and ruined the whole visit! I think we are that way in Africa sometimes. We try to minister before we have listened, and before we have learned enough from them.

Willing to Suffer

Are you willing to suffer for Africa? Are you willing literally and personally to suffer in order to win the battle there? If you are willing, you *can* do so, and you *will* do so, even if you never leave your own hometown.

I have said earlier that the primary ministry which God has given me over the years is to the suffering church. I feel very strongly about the responsibility of Christians in freedom to minister to those in bondage. God must feel that way too. As a heavenly Father, He must be especially inclined toward those of His children who are hurting. I have five children and I love them all equally. But if one were sick and suffering, my wife and I would pay attention to that suffering one. That would be an appropriate priority. So it is with God's children. Not only would a loving God not neglect those children who are suffering; He actually would lend a special grace to them.

Half the world's population is behind barbed wire today, living in countries where their worship is challenged and their freedom restricted. It is obscene for those of us in free countries to be so absorbed in ourselves that we forget our suffering brothers and sisters. We must tell them that we love them, that every day of our lives we are thinking about them. We must get the message through to those prisons in Mozambique, and those who fear for their lives in Angola—we must *show* them all that they are not written off, that we are upholding them before the Lord. We must get through to them, even if it means crossing borders illegally, with Bibles, material goods, and fellowship. We must remind them that they and we both belong to the Body of Christ, and that they are not forgotten.

There cannot be two kinds of Christians—those who pay a price and those who do not—those who live in hardship and those who live in luxury—those who carry the cross and those who "sail on flowery beds of ease." If we are truly children of God, we must be willing to share the suffering of the imprisoned church. We must be willing to minister to them by suffering with them. It is not good enough just to pray for the suffering church in a perfunctory manner, as if it were merely one more item on a long laundry list of prayer requests. The Bible teaches that we can actually pray for our suffering brethren in such a way that we vicariously suffer *with them!* We who live in free countries have not had suffering forced on us, but we nevertheless can choose to suffer vicariously with those who have! We can so identify with our suffering brethren that we actually suffer in our own spirits. (Read Hebrews 10:32, 33.)

This is a message of hope for the middle-class, overblessed Western church. So many of us have had so much, such an abundance of liberty and comfort. We virtually wallow in the "good life" of the West, and when we hear about the terrible suffering that others endure, we feel guilty and embarrassed by the multitude of our blessings. But it is not constructive to feel guilty. You cannot help it if you were born in America. You cannot run down to the nearest jail and ask the jailer to lock you up for the sake of the church. But there *is* something constructive you can do. You can ask God to so burden you with the needs of Africa that you actually suffer, *literally* suffer. Are you willing to do that? Are you willing for God to make you feel, painfully feel, the grief of Mary Luwum tonight as you try to sleep? Are you willing to feel the fear of Christians in hiding, or the loneliness of those who are in exile?

If you are willing to suffer with the suffering church, then your prayer on their behalf will reach God's heart. Only then. Intercessory prayer is a potent force. It is a real power, but only when it accompanies the commitment I have just described. Will your prayers of intercession actually make things better for the church in Africa? Of course they will! The Bible even indicates (Hebrews 13:3, 18, 19) that intercessory prayer can get people out of jail. The length of the sentence is not determined by the judge—though he may think it is—but by praying Christians. To pray effective intercessory prayers, it is not enough to pray once-over-lightly, without focusing on what one is doing. Sit still; block out other distracting thoughts; wait until you can actually visualize that person in a jail cell—or wherever—then pray for him as if he were your own son or father. God will answer that kind of prayer.

That kind of prayer comes when you have chosen to become one with your suffering brother. We are all members of the same body. When a man is hit on the soles of his feet, his tongue cries out. In Africa Christians are being hit, tortured, tormented; but they cannot speak, so we must speak for them. We must cry out. We must weep with them, pray with them, fast for them—if possible, even go to them.

Does it do any good? When Aida Skripnikova was in prison in Leningrad, sentenced to three years for distributing gospel literature, we sent her a small box of chocolate. The prison authorities told her about the gift when it arrived, but refused to give it to her. When she talked with us after being released, she said that hearing about the chocolate we sent was as good as getting it, simply because she knew others cared. That did more good than the chocolate. I believe in the value of intercession because I have sometimes been on the receiving end. I have had moments when I was down, or sick, or tired; and suddenly, with no apparent reason, I got an uplift, a physical touch, a spiritual lift. I knew that somewhere—right at that moment—someone was praying for me, and God was hearing. God will answer the prayer you pray, and transmit your strength to your suffering brother. But first you must be willing to suffer with him.

Willing to Give

How can you help win the battle for Africa? By giving, of course.

But before you reach for your checkbook, let me explain the kind of giving I speak of. I do not mean giving money by itself. I don't think God has much appreciation for "checkbook Christians," who just peel money off the top of their bank accounts and drop it into a missions envelope because that is the easiest thing to do. For God to honor a gift, and make maximum use of it, the giver must be personally involved in it.

Americans are the most generous people in the world. Too generous, I think. They are so big-hearted and sentimental that they sometimes give emotionally, and not intelligently. Someone makes an appeal that touches them emotionally and they automatically reach for their wallets. But just to give is not good enough. We must give freely, to be sure, but still give strategically and as a result of prayer. It doesn't make sense, if we recognize the African battle as a spiritual one, to give always for poverty, food, and orphans more willingly than we give for evangelism. We must be clearheaded enough to give for the purpose of changing the system, not just to feed a hungry child. We must find out *why* he is hungry, and go to the root of it. We must work on the causes, not deal with the symptoms only.

The Communists never give food to hungry people. Lenin said that the Revolution should not give money to a beggar, but rather make him poorer so he will revolt against the system that impoverished him. Address yourself to his spirit, and not his belly. There is a valuable lesson in strategic giving there. We must give our money to those things that will make a permanent difference. Give him the Gospel; give him the truth; give him something for his spirit as you feed his body.

I believe in giving, but not willy-nilly, sentimental giving that has not been prayed over. I have had God tell me on a particular day to give whatever I am asked for on that day. And I do it. Sometimes as I am praying in the morning, the Holy Spirit will bring to mind the Scripture from Matthew 5:42 that says to give to him that asks. When that happens, someone always asks me for something, and I know that I am to give it to him. It always happens. Once in Berlin I was praying with a group of refugees in a small devotional group. In our prayers together one night this verse came to me. On the way home, as I walked along a dark back street, a man came out of the shadows and asked for my money. I was not the least bit surprised; I just put my hand in my pocket and gave him my money. I don't know if he was drunk or a thief or what, and I don't really care. I know God for some reason wanted him to have my money. And as I walked on I said, "Praise the Lord!" because it showed me that God was taking me seriously.

One day when I was in Bible school I had the same leading, and that day a fellow student asked me for my accordion. I had always wanted an accordion for myself, and had not owned this one long, but I gave it to him and felt wonderful about it. At a missionary convention last year the same impression came to me, and I wound up giving my shoes to a fellow missionary. They fit him perfectly, as it turned out, and I walked back to my hotel room in my socks. Another time a Cuban pastor was seeing me off at the airport in Havana. As I started to leave, I felt led to ask him:

"What do you need most, brother?"

"I need a pair of shoes."

"Praise the Lord, brother! They are yours!"

And I took off my shoes, handed them to him, and padded into the plane in my stockinged feet for the flight to Europe. As I left, there sounded over and over in my mind the last words of that man when I gave him the shoes. "Now you have given everything, Andrew," he said earnestly. "The only thing you have left to give is your life!"

The critical thing about giving is that it be personal, and it be the result of God's guidance. I have a rule of thumb by which I judge if my giving is of God. I ask myself, "Andrew, are you willing to help in *any* way God calls on you to help?" That may mean going personally to a foreign field. It may mean committing yourself as a teacher or a technician or a missionary. But whatever God wants you to do to help Africa, are you willing to do it? If you are truly willing to go yourself, and then God says, "No, don't go. Instead give this amount of money," then okay, give it and the Lord will bless you. But not if you just give to ease your guilt, or just to say you have done your part. If you are genuinely willing to help in any way God calls on you to help, and He calls on you to help by giving your money—then that is the way to give.

Willing to Go

That brings us to the toughest demand of all: you can make an impact in the battle for Africa if you are willing to go there yourself. It is at this point that everyone begins to say, "Who? Me?" Almost everyone who reads this book will think that going—actually, personally *going* to Africa—is for him an absurd suggestion and not at all possible.

But is it?

Most people can make enough money in five years to stretch it out over six, if they cut down to simple necessities. Why not bank one-fifth of your income for five years, and spend that sixth year working for no pay in Africa, living off those savings? There are literally hundreds of thousands of Christian schoolteachers in the English-speaking world who could teach in Africa for two years. It would not be as comfortable as life at home, but the opportunity *is* there. When construction began on the Alaskan pipeline, the word went out that technicians and laborers could make extremely high wages there. To get the money, they had to endure horrible living conditions, bitter cold, separation from their families, but still men poured into Alaska by the thousands. Are Christians less willing to suffer hardship for the Kingdom than sinners are for the dollar?

In almost all the universities in Africa, teachers are being sought to fill open positions. The London *Times* contains advertisements every week from so-called "closed" African countries seeking lecturers for their universities. A Christian educator cannot get into those countries as a missionary, but he can as a lecturer, and likewise for many different types of engineers, technicians, and professional men. Certainly that strategy of evangelism is not unknown to the Revolution. Throughout the underdeveloped countries of the world, white radical university professors have seized the opportunity to influence African and Asian students. They have seen those advertisements and responded to them. Why do we not do the same? The doors that are "closed" to the church are often wide open to individual Christians. The era of traditional missionary work may be soon over in Africa. My sons have told me they want to be missionaries. I tell them, "No. Learn a trade first, then you can go with something to offer the people which will make them want to listen to your Gospel."

Young people in a rally in Peking once were seen carrying banners with the slogan: GO WHERE THE REVOLUTION NEEDS YOU MOST! That should be the challenge of the Christian Gospel: *Go where the Kingdom needs you most!* Are you willing to help in the battle for Africa, even if it means moving there personally? For young people especially, there are many expanding ministries (Operation Mobilization, Youth With a Mission, Campus Crusade for Christ, Wycliffe Bible Translators, for example) which need workers, and can place you (though with little pay) in a strategic area in Africa where your presence can be felt. One thing is certain: If you have a burden for Africa, and you are willing to go personally, *whatever the cost,* God will find a way to get you in. He does not burden men frivolously.

Rev. Walter Ciszek was a Jesuit priest who spent twenty-three years in a Siberian concentration camp. He could have gotten out earlier, but he chose to stay as a witness to other prisoners who needed the Gospel. I have known of Chinese Christians who have gone into Red China with the specific intention of being arrested and imprisoned so that they could preach and witness to the Chinese in the jails. "It is easy to get into China," they have said, "if one is willing not to come out again." That is the brand of revolutionary Christian discipleship that can overpower any Revolution of man's making.

White Africans should ask themselves, "Is it possible that someday we could be sold into black Africa as slaves? And would we accept that, if it came, and seize it as an opportunity, painful as it would be, to evangelize Africa?" And westerners need to ask themselves, "Would we be willing—if there were no other way—to give up our liberty and our way of life in order to take the Gospel to Russia and China as a conquered nation?" Only when we are willing to embrace something that extreme—only when we are willing for *anything* in order to win the world—only when we drop all conditions and say simply, "Lord, I will *go* . . ."—only then will we be sure that the battle for Africa cannot possibly be lost.

That is a tough challenge. I don't know if I am up to it. But I pray daily that God will put me and keep me in that position of willingness. Like Abraham at the sacrifice of Isaac, I know that when I am at that point of being ready for total sacrifice, then I am ready for Him to use me.

And then we can face the people of Africa and say to them with total honesty: "We want to be your servants and not your masters. We know the history of your land, and we are sorry for it; but, praise the Lord, we don't have to stop there. We can go on to say we love you and we show our love by sharing with you side by side in the work of the Kingdom."

And together, by the Lord's strong arm, we will win the battle for Africa for the Kingdom of God!

If you wish to write to Brother Andrew,
address your letters to:

Open Doors With Brother Andrew
Post Office Box 2040
Orange, CA 92669

Appendix

A country-by-country description of sub-Saharan Africa, with the position of each on the African map indicated, and information on each nation. Compiled by the research staff of Open Doors International.

TUNISIA
MOROCCO
WESTERN SAHARA
ALGERIA
LIBYA
EGYPT
MAURITANIA
MALI
NIGER
CHAD
SUDAN
DJIBOUTI
UPPER VOLTA
NIGERIA
ETHIOPIA
GUINEA
SIERRA LEONE
LIBERIA
IVORY COAST
GHANA
TOGO
BENIN
CENT. AFRICAN REP.
SOMALIA
CAMEROON
EQUATORIAL GUINEA
GABON
CONGO
UGANDA
KENYA
RWANDA
ZAIRE
BURUNDI
TANZANIA
MALAWI
ANGOLA
ZAMBIA
MOZAMBIQUE
MADAGASCAR
RHODESIA
SOUTH WEST AFRICA
BOTSWANA
SWAZILAND
SOUTH AFRICA
LESOTHO

ANGOLA
Population: 6.4 million

481,351 square miles
Capital: Luanda

95% African, 1% European, 2% mestizos
Major Tribes: Ovimbundu 38%, Kimbundu 23%, Bacongo 13%
Religion: 16% Christians, animists
Literacy rate: 20%
One-party People's Republic
Popular Movement for Liberation of Angola (MPLA)
President: Agostino Neto

BENIN
Population: 3.1 million

43,483 square miles
Capital: Porto-Novo

99% African
Religion: 65% animists, 15% Christians, 13% Muslim
One-party Republic
President: Lt. Colonel Mathieu Kerekou

BOTSWANA 238,805 square miles
Population: 693,000 Capital: Gaborone

94% African, 8 main tribal groups: Bangwato, Bakweno, Batawana, Bangwaketse, Bakgatla, Bamalete, Barolong, Batlokwa
Religion: 85% animists, 15% Christians
Literacy rate: 33% in Setswana, 25% in English
One-party Republic (March 1965)
National Assembly
President: Sir Seretse Khama

BURUNDI 10,744 square miles
Population: 4.1 million Capital: Bujumbura

99% African
Major Tribes: Hutu 85%, Tutsi 14%, Twa 1%
Religion: Christian 60%, animists and Muslim
Literacy: 55%
One-party Republic (1 July, 1962)
National Party of Unity and Progress (UPRONA)
Col. Jean-Baptiste Bagaza

CAMEROON
183,568 square miles
Population: 6.4 million
Capital: Yaoundé

200 tribes
Religion: Islam, Christianity, animists
Literacy: 65%
One-party Republic (1 January, 1960)
National Cameroonian Union (UNC)
President: Ahmadou Ahidjo

CENTRAL AFRICAN REPUBLIC
242,000 square miles
Population: 2.4 million
Capital: Bangui

Ethnic Groups: Baya-Mandija and Banda 66%, M'baka 7%, 80 other groups
Religion: Protestant 40%, Catholic 28%, animist 24%, Muslim 8%
Literacy: 18%
One-party Republic (13 August, 1960)
Movement d'Evolution Sociale en Afrique Noire (MESAN)
President: Jean-Bédel Bokassa (Since this book was prepared for publication, President Bokassa has been crowned Emperor.)

CHAD
Population: 4.2 million

496,000 square miles
Capital: N'Djamena

99% African
Ethnic Groups: Sudanic Group (Sara, Banana, Moundang, Baguirmian), Nilotic Group (Ouaddian, Dar Massalit, Moubi, Dadjo), Arab Group (Hassaouna, Djoheina), Saharan Group (Kanimbou, Toubou)
Religion: Islam majority, animist, Christian 5%
Literacy: 10%
Military Government (11 August, 1960)
Supreme Military Committee (SMC)
President: Felix Malloum

CONGO, REPUBLIC OF (Brazzaville)
Population: 1.4 million

132,000 square miles
Capital: Brazzaville

99% African
Major Tribes: Bakongo, Bateke, M'Bochi, Sangha
Religion: animists 48%, Christian 47%, Muslim 5%
Literacy: 20%
One-party People's Republic (15 August, 1960)
Congolese Labor Party (PCT)
11-man military junta (as of 31 March, 1977)

DJIBOUTI (formerly the French Territory of the Afars and the Issas, formerly French Somaliland)
Population: 150,000
8,800 square miles
Capital: Djibouti

Tribal Groups: Afars, Issas
Religion: predominantly Muslim
French territorial government (1967)
Independent state (1977)

EQUATORIAL GUINEA
Population: 350,000
10,820 square miles
Capital: Santa Isabel

98% African
Tribal Groups: Fangs 75%, Benges, Combes, Bujebas, Balenges, Fernandinos, Bubis
Religion: Catholic 60%, Protestant, animist
Literacy: 20%
One-party Republic (12 October, 1968)
Partido Unico National (PUN)
President: Francisco Macias Nguema

ETHIOPIA
Population: 29.5 million

472,000 square miles
Capital: Addis Ababa

99% African
Ethnic Groups: Amhara 25%, Galla 40%, Tigre 12%, Sidama 9%, Somali 2%
Religion: Ethiopian Orthodox Christian 40%, Muslim 40%, animist 20%
Literacy: 7%
Military Government (1975)
Provisional Military Administrative Council (PMAC)
Colonel Mengistu Haile Mariam

GABON
Population: 575,000

102,317 square miles
Capital: Libreville

98% African
Major Tribes: Fang, Eshira, Bapounou, Bateke, Okanda
Religion: Christian 46%, Muslim, animist, fetishist
Literacy: 20%
One-party Republic (17 August, 1960)
Gabonese Democratic Party (PDG)
President: Albert Bernard Bongo

GAMBIA
Population: 550,000
4,003 square miles
Capital: Banjul

98% African
Tribal Groups: Mandingo 40%, Fula 13%, Wolof 12%, Jola 7%, Serahuli 7%
Religion: Muslim 85%, animist and Christian 15%
Literacy: 10%
Two-party Republic (18 February, 1965)
Progressive People's Party (PPP), United Party (UP)
President: Dawda Kairaba Jawara

GHANA
Population: 11 million
92,100 square miles
Capital: Accra

99% African
Major Tribes: Akan, Ewe, Ga
Religion: animists 45%, Christian 43%, Muslim 12%
Literacy: 25%
Military government (1957)
Supreme Military Council (SMC)
General I. K. Acheampong

GUINEA
Population: 4.6 million
95,000 square miles
Capital: Conakry

Ethnic Groups: Foulah, Malinke, Soussous
Religion: Muslim 75%, animist 24%, Christian 1%
Literacy: 10%
One-party Republic (2 October, 1958)
Democratic Party of Guinea (PDG)
President: Ahmed Sékou Touré

GUINEA-BISSAU
Population: 750,000
14,000 square miles
Capital: Bissau

97% African
Major Tribes: Balanta 30%, Fulani 20%, Mandyako 14%, Malinke 13%, Papel 7%
Religion: animist 69%, Muslim 30%, Christian 1%
Literacy: 5%
One-party Republic (10 September, 1974)
African Party for Independence of G-Biss, and Cape Verde (PAIGC)
President: Luis de Almeida Cabral

IVORY COAST
124,500 square miles
Population: 6.5 million
Capital: Abidjan

96% African
Over 60 tribes
Religion: animists 63%, Muslim 25%, Christian 12%
Literacy: 20%
One-party Republic (7 August, 1960)
Parti Democratique de la Côte dîvoire (PDCI)
President: Félix Houpouët-Boigny

KENYA
224,900 square miles
Population: 14.1 million
Capital: Nairobi

98% African, 1.1% Asian, 0.9% other
125 tribes: Kikuku 20%, Luo 15%, Abaluhya 13%, Kamba 11%, Kisii 6%, Meru 5%, other 30%
Religion: animists 38%, Protestant 37%, Roman Catholic 22%, Muslim 3%
Literacy: 24%
One-party Republic (1964)
President: Jomo Kenyatta

LESOTHO — 11,716 square miles
Population: 1,125,000 — Capital: Maseru

Tribes: mostly Basotho
Religion: 50% Christian, other traditional, animist
Literacy: 50%
Constitutional monarchy
King: Motlotlehi Moshoeshoe II (1969)
Prime Minister: Leabua Jonathan

LIBERIA — 43,000 square miles
Population: 1.6 million — Capital: Monrovia

Ethnic Groups: 16 tribes (97.5%, principally Mande, West Atlantic, and Kwa), Americo-Liberians (2.5%)
Religion: tribal religions 70–80%, Muslim 10–20%, Christian 10%
Literacy: 10%
One-party Republic (1847)
True Whig Party
President: William R. Tolbert, Jr.

LIBYA — 679,360 square miles
Population: 3 million — Capital: Tripoli

Ethnic Groups: Arabs and Arabized Berbers 97%, Negroes
Religion: Sunni Islam
Literacy: 27–35%
Military Republic (24 December 1951)
Revolutionary Command Council (RCC)
Chairman Col. Mu'ammar al-Qadhafi

MALAGASY (Madagascar) — 228,000 square miles
Population: 9 million — Capital: Tananarive

Ethnic Groups: 18 Malagasy tribes; 40,000 Comoran islanders, 6,000 French, 17,000 Indians; 9,000 Chinese
Religion: Christian, animists
Literacy: 40%
Military Republic (26 June 1960)
Supreme Revolutionary Council
President: Cdr. Didier Ratsiraka

MALAWI 45,747 square miles
Population: 5.3 million Capital: Lilongwe

98% African
Tribal Groups: Chewas, Nyanja, Lomwe, Yao, Sena, Tumbuka
Religion: traditional, Christianity, Islam
Literacy: 25%
One-party Republic (6 July, 1964)
Malawi Congress Party (MCP)
President: Hastings Kamuzu Banda

MALI 464,873 square miles
Population: 5.91 million Capital: Bamako

Ethnic Groups: Mandé (Bambara, Malinké, Sarakollé) 50%, Peul 17.2%, Voltaic 12.2%, Songhai 5.6%, Tuareg and Moors 4.6%
Religion: 90% Islam, 9% indigenous, 1% Christian
Literacy: under 5%
Military Republic (September 22, 1960)
Military Committee of National Liberation (MCNL)
President: Col. Moussa Traoré

MAURITANIA
419,229 square miles
Population: 1.5 million
Capital: Nouakchott

Ethnic Groups: Arab-Berber 80%, Negroid 20%
Religion: Islam 99%
Literacy: 6%
One-party Constitutional (28 November, 1960)
Mauritanian Peoples Party (MPP)
President: Moktar Ould Daddah

MOZAMBIQUE
303,769 square miles
Population: 9.1 million
Capital: Maputo

99.4% African, .6% other (many tribes)
Religion: animists 65%, Christian 22%, Muslim 11%
Literacy: 20%
One-party People's Republic (25 June, 1975)
FRELIMO (Frente de Liberacion Mocambique)
President: Samora Machel

NIGER
490,000 square miles
Population: 4.9 million
Capital: Niamey

99% African
Major Tribes: Hausa 50%, Djermas 23%, Fulanis 15%, Tuaregs 12%
Religion: mostly Muslim, few animists and Christians
Literacy: 6%
Military government (3 August, 1960)
Supreme Military Council (SMC)
Col. Seyni Kountche

NIGERIA
357,000 square miles
Population: 64.7 million
Capital: Lagos

250 tribes, Hausi-Fulani, Ibo, Yourba 60%
Religion: 47% Muslim, 34.5% Christian, 18.5% animist and other
Literacy: 25%
Federal Republic (Oct. 1, 1963)
Federal Military Government (FMG) 1966
Commander-in-Chief: Lt.-General Olusegun Obasanjo.

RHODESIA (ZIMBABWE) 150,333 square miles
Population: 6.6 million Capital: Salisbury

96% African, 3% European, 1% Asians & coloreds
Religion: 51% syncretic (part Christian–part animist), 25% Christian, 24% animist, some Muslim
Literacy: 30% African, 100% European and Asian
Multi-party Republic (UDI 1965)
Prime Minister: Ian D. Smith

RWANDA 10,169 square miles
Population: 4.3 million Capital: Kigali

99% African
Tribal Groups: Hutu 89%, Tutsi 10%, Twa 1%, 3,000 Asians, 2,000 Europeans, 150 Americans
Religion: animists, Christian, Muslim
Literacy: 15%
Military Government (1 July, 1962)
Committee for National Peace and Unity
Major General Juvenal Habyarimana

SENEGAL — 76,000 square miles
Population: 4.5 million — Capital: Dakar

99% African
Major Tribes: Wolof 36%, Peuhl 18%, Serere 17%, Toucouleur 9%, Diola 9%, Mandingo 6%
Religion: Muslim 80%, Christian, animist
Literacy: 8%
Two-party Republic (4 April, 1960)
Union Progressiste Senegalaise (UPS), Parti Democratique Senegalaise (PDS)
Léopold-Sédar Senghor

SIERRA LEONE — 27,925 square miles
Population: 2.8 million — Capital: Freetown

98% African
Major Tribes: Temne 30%, Mende 30%
Religion: animist 70%, Muslim 25%, Christian 5%
Literacy: 10%
Two-party Republic (27 April 1961)
All People's Congress (APC)
Sierra Leone People's Party (SLPP)
President: Siaka P. Stevens

SOMALIA
246,155 square miles
Population: 3.3 million
Capital: Mogadiscio

98.8% Somali, 1.2% Arab and Asian
Religion: Muslim 99%, other 1%
Literacy: 20%
Military Government (1 July, 1960)
Supreme Revolutionary Council (SRC)
Major General Mohammed Siad Barre

SOUTH AFRICA
472,494 square miles
Population: 26.3 million
Capital: Pretoria (Administrative)
Cape Town (Legislative)

Africans 70–75%, Zulu 5 million, Xhosa 4.9 million
Religion: Dutch Reformed, Reformed Church of S.A. Anglicans, Methodists, Presbyterians, Roman Catholics, Jews, Baptists, and Syncretic (part Christian–part animist)
Democratic Central Government but elected by whites only. There are four mainstream political parties for whites. The blacks have no direct representation in the white parliament. There are various homelands for blacks where black govern black. Two of these homelands were independent by 1977 but not recognized by the outside world.
State President: Dr. N. Diederichs
Prime Minister: B. J. Vorster

SOUTH WEST AFRICA (Namibia) — 318,261 square miles
Population: 915,000 — Capital: Windhoek

85% African, 15% Europeans
Major Tribes: Ovambo, Dama, Herero, Nama or Hottentot, Okavango, East Caprivian, Cape Coloureds, Rehoboth Basters, Bushman, Kaokovelder, Tswana
Religion: Animists, Lutheran, Roman Catholic, Methodists, Anglican and Dutch Reformed
Literacy: Less than 10%
Governed by a Legislative Assembly responsible to South Africa. In 1977 negotiations with Western Powers on independence for this mandate territory were approaching a final stage.
Political groups: National Party (whites), Turnhalle Alliance, Swapo
Administrator General: Judge M. T. Steyn

SPANISH SAHARA — 102,703 square miles
Population: 92,750 — Capital: El Aaiún

Spanish, Arab, Berber, Negro
Religion: Muslim, Catholic
Literacy: 100% Europeans, 5% Nomads
One-party Republic
The National Movement (TNM)
Governor General and Commanding Officer: Brigadier Gen. Jose Maria Perez De Lema Tejero

SUDAN
Population: 18.2 million
967,500 square miles
Capital: Khartoum

Arabian, African Tribes: Dinka, Nuer, Smilluk
Religion: Islam, 4% Christian, animists
Literacy: 10–15%
Military Dictatorship
Sudanese Socialist Union (SSU)
President: Jafar Muhammad Nimeri

SWAZILAND
Population: 534,250
6,705 square miles
Capital: Mbabane (Mod. Administration)
Lobamba (Traditional/Legis.)

96% African
Tribes: Swazi 96%, Zulu and Shangane
Religion: 57% Christian, 43% animist
Languages: Swazi and English
Literacy: 30%
One-party Republic (Feb. 1968)
Imbokodvo Movement
Chief of State: King Sobhuza II

TANZANIA
363,950 square miles
Population: 15.6 million
Capital: Dar es Salaam

99% African, 1% Indo-Pakistanis, Arabs and Europeans
Over 130 Tribes, mainly Sukuma and Myamwezi
Religion: Christian 35%, Muslim 35%, animists 30%
Literacy: 45–50%
One-party Republic
Tanganyika African National Union (TANU)
Afro-Shirazi Party (ASP)
President: Julius K. Nyerere

TOGO
21,853 square miles
Population: 2.4 million
Capital: Lomé

99% African
Major Tribes: Ewe, Mina, Kabyé
Religion: animist 75%, Christian 20%, Muslim 5%
Literacy: 10%
One-party Republic (27 April, 1960)
Rassemblement de Peuple Togolias (RPT)
General Gnassingbé Eyadéma

UGANDA 91,070 square miles
Population: 12.1 million Capital: Kampala

99% African
Major Groups: Bantu, Nilotic, Niol-Hamitic, Sudanic
Religion: Christian 60%, Muslim 6%, animist and other
Literacy: 30%
Military Government (9 October, 1962)
No parties
General Idi Amin Dada

UPPER VOLTA 106,000 square miles
Population: 6 million Capital: Ouagadougou

99% African
Tribal Groups: Mossi, Bobo, Mande
Religion: animists, Muslim, Christian
Literacy: 10%
Military Government (1960)
No parties
Major General Aboubakar Sangoule Lamizana

ZAIRE 905,063 square miles
Population: 27.2 million Capital: Kinshasa

80% Bantu (over 200 tribal groups)
Religion: 50% Catholic and Protestant, Kimbanguism, syncretic sects, traditional religions
Literacy: 35%
Presidential, one-party (30 June, 1960)
The Popular Movement of the Revolution (MPR)
President: Mobutu Sese Seko

ZAMBIA 290,724 square miles
Population: 5.2 million Capital: Lusaka

98% African
Mainly Bantu tribes
Religion: animists and Christian
Literacy: 20%
One-party Republic (24 October, 1964)
United National Independence Party (UNIP)
President: Kenneth Kaunda